FEED MY SHEEP

Essays in Pastoral Theology

EDITED BY

FRANCIS UNDERHILL, M.A.

Warden of Liddon House

A. R. MOWBRAY & CO. LTD.
LONDON : 28 Margaret Street, Oxford Circus, W. 1
OXFORD : 9 High Street
MILWAUKEE, U.S.A, : The Morehouse Publishing Co.
Printed in England

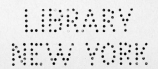

First impression, 1927

EDITOR'S PREFACE

THE essays contained in this book represent an attempt to set forth briefly some aspects of the pastoral method employed by those who would claim in the widest sense the name of Anglo-Catholic. The writers are men who have had considerable experience in practical work.

It has not been possible to meet for conference, and it is likely that on minor points different views might be held among us, but in main outline we should agree as to means of edification and sanctification.

The book is intended not so much as a series of instructions as an explanation of certain ways of getting to work. It is hoped that it may satisfy those who in general agree with the writers, and lead to a better understanding between ourselves and those who have the same ends in view but approach them somewhat differently.

FRANCIS UNDERHILL.

CONTENTS

THE PRIEST OF TO-DAY

By Francis Underhill

I

THE PRIEST OF TO-DAY

THE preface to the Ordination Service in the Prayer Book contains the following passage :

It is evident unto all men diligently reading holy Scripture and ancient Authors, that from the Apostles' time there have been these Orders of Ministers in Christ's Church ; Bishops, Priests, and Deacons. . . . And therefore, to the intent that these Orders may be continued, and reverently used and esteemed, in the Church of England ; no man shall be accounted or taken to be a lawful Bishop, Priest, or Deacon . . . except he be called, tried, examined, and admitted thereunto, according to the Form hereafter following.

So throughout the Christian ages the Church has set apart men and ordained them for a special function. She entrusts to them certain divine powers which belong to the holy body of Christ, but which, for convenience sake, must be exercised in her name by her appointed servants. But, as S. Paul says, they are more than servants of the Church—they are the ministers of Christ and stewards of the mysteries of God. Their duties are to teach the Faith by virtue of the authority of Christ in the Church, and to minister the Sacraments ordained by Christ and continued in His

3

mystical Body. Such is the Christian ministry, and such is the commission entrusted to the priest to be exercised on behalf of his fellow members of the Church.

In view of so high and responsible a vocation, it is strange to notice the curious unpopularity of priesthood in general, which shows itself in a certain distrust of the individual priest. It is true indeed that a faithful minister of the Church, by virtue of his office, gains a trust and affection from those he serves which is quite unique. That is his consolation for the suspicion he meets from those who are outside his influence. This feeling is shown in strange little ways. For instance, a priest can be pretty sure of keeping a railway carriage empty, unless the train be very crowded, by merely sitting there wearing a clerical collar; while in many other relations of life a priest is conscious that he has a certain initial difficulty to surmount before people begin to trust and like him. This is peculiar to his office ; he must accept it with all that it means.

The causes of this suspicion are not easy to trace. It cannot be denied, however, that the fault has often lain, and sometimes still lies, with the priesthood itself. There has often in history been very firm ground for political mistrust of priests. Nor is this reproach yet entirely removed. Government by priests for some reason has seldom been good for the governed, while individual priests have sometimes debased the spiritual power entrusted to them into personal tyranny. They have substituted human dominion for spiritual direction. These and other dangers and mistakes may help to account for the curious condition of a fairly large part of the public mind as regards the clergy, but they do not wholly explain it. There is, and must always be, something inherent in the idea of the priesthood which antagonizes certain elements in human nature. Rooted in the whole conception of the Church, and lying beyond the personal ministry of the Church, is the sense of an authority not of this world, demanding no less than the surrender of the whole personality of each man to the claims of Christ. This can never be abated, and it probably accounts, unconsciously, for a good deal of the antagonism which men and women feel.

THE STANDARD DEMANDED OF THE MODERN PRIEST

This same sense appears conversely in the very high standard of life rightly expected from the priest by the laity. Probably this demand was never higher in England than it is to-day. The clergyman must be a person of absolutely unimpeachable moral life. Whatever excuses may be made for the erring layman, and many are made, little toleration is shown towards the sinful priest. Every newspaper takes up the story of the scandal ; it is discussed in every

club and public-house ; everybody is shocked.
We dare not complain of this. Indeed we can
only be thankful that so high an ideal is expected
of us.

The standard is high, and we are upheld by
the knowledge that we bear with us far more
than our own personal reputation. Men judge
the whole Church of God and the claims of our
Lord Jesus Christ by our life and actions. We
may well be thankful for the growing demand
made by the laity for a spiritual priesthood.
The days are long past when Mr. Collins and
his parishioners thought that he had well fulfilled his duty when he had expressed his
' earnest endeavour to demean himself with
grateful respect towards her ladyship, and be
ever ready to perform those rites and ceremonies which are instituted by the Church of
England.' There may be fewer lay people
practising Christianity nowadays than there
were a hundred years ago, but those who
do care for their religion are learning great
things about the spiritual life. Any incon-
sistency which would appear to show that the
priest is ' just like other people ' is severely
viewed by the laity, even though it may mean
no more than that he is just an ordinary man.

The new knowledge and literature of prayer
which mark our times lay upon parish priests
everywhere the duty of being themselves
sufficiently men of prayer to be able to advise
others. This is a very grave responsibility.

We do not want to fail our people here at the highest point of their spiritual life. The trouble is that laymen and laywomen tend to set the standard almost impossibly high for their clergy, and to be too severe when they find that the priest, too, has his weaknesses. The true teaching that ' the unworthiness of the ministers . . . hinders not the effect of the Sacrament ' [1] is too often forgotten, and men make the imperfection of the priest an excuse for forsaking their Church and lowering the standard of their own lives. Never were the clergy so intently watched as they are in our days. Men whose belief in Christianity is almost non-existent, and whose attachment to the Christian ideal is very slight, yet look for great things from the clergy. But again let us be glad that the standard is almost perilously high.

A demand of yet another kind is made upon priests by some members of their congregations. The need for obvious holiness and sufficient learning are dealt with in other essays contained in this volume. It is only necessary to say here that while a large number of members of every congregation are consciously, or thoughtlessly, traditional in their view of Christian doctrine, there are also men and women, particularly the young, who expect their priest to be aware of the criticisms and objections which are brought against orthodox Christianity

[1] Article xxvi.

to-day. Without expecting him to be a
'modernist'—whatever that term may mean
—they do expect him to possess a modern
mind.

Less worthy than this is the unexpressed
demand, especially in the country, that the
priest shall be prosperous, able to furnish his
house well, and to entertain his parishioners
and friends. It is to be feared that the poverty
of many of the clergy does not always call out
respect and sympathy from their people. I
do not know the life of country places very well,
but I am assured by many who do that the hard
lot of the clergy who suffer from the new
poverty is sometimes made harder by the
scarcely veiled contempt they have to bear.
This may be exaggeration. I hope so. But
at any rate the whole social position of many
of the clergy is undergoing a profound alteration.

Yet, in spite of all this, and in face of the
bitterness of the struggle which is the lot of
many priests to-day, the laity rightly demand
a special courtesy and charity of manner from
their clergy. A priest may be ever so hard put
to it, but he must not be quarrelsome. The
layman may lose his temper, and little is thought
of it. Not so the priest. A sudden exclama-
tion, or a quick little flash of anger when
provocation is almost unbearable, may undo the
patient work of years. Whatever change may
come over the circumstances of the priesthood,

it may be taken for certain that in no smallest degree will the standard expected of the clergy by the laity be lowered. It will probably tend constantly to rise.

THE DUTIES OF THE PRIEST

If that is so, then we must turn to the consideration of some of the general duties of the English priest to whom is committed the ministry of the Word and the Sacraments. The former will be briefly considered elsewhere under the heading of 'Preaching.' It may be well to dwell for a little here on certain primary aspects of the priestly life as they concern the administration of the Sacraments. Ordered liberty is vital to the Church ; but it must be confessed that liberty has of late years gone far enough in England. A movement towards uniformity of rite is imperative. And first of all we may surely look as a result of revision of the Prayer Book for a movement towards uniformity in the manner in which the clergy celebrate the Holy Eucharist.

It is no business of ours to interfere with the methods adopted by our Evangelical friends, though it is greatly to be hoped that in some not too far distant future an ' English use ' may be evolved on which we may all be able to agree. In the meantime, we who are known as Anglo-Catholics shall certainly be called upon to reduce our various individual habits to some one normal standard. This consideration seems to come in here more naturally than in the essay on 'Public Worship' because it so specially concerns each priest of the English Church.

It is no fault of ours to-day that confusion has arisen. All right-minded men deplore it, but many of us may have to suffer the abandonment of details to which we have long grown accustomed in our manner of saying Mass. Many of these things may be in themselves small, but no detail is unimportant which is seen by the worshipping congregation. It is not claimed that even the setting forth of the revised Prayer Book will be immediately followed by the adoption of one rite for the whole English Church. That, unhappily, is more than the most hopeful of us can look for. But Anglo-Catholics should aim at arriving among themselves at uniformity of rite and ceremonial, even at the cost of sacrifice. Our self-denial might lead the way to the general reform which is so urgently needed and so long overdue. This must be done primarily for the sake of the laity. It is surely deplorable that any and every priest should in practice be his own Ordinary ; so that no English layman entering one of our churches to hear Mass can be in any way sure of what he will see and hear ; indeed whether he will hear at all. Thousands of laymen are lost to the Catholic Movement every year simply because when they come to our services they have not the least idea what is going on. If we are ever to win England, we *must* give the laity the Book of Common Prayer. A few can be trained in other ways. The great majority will always want ' the book.'

Side by side with the need for reform in the manner of celebrating goes the necessity that every priest should be instructed in the right administration of the Sacrament of Penance, popularly known as Confession and Absolution. This matter will also be dealt with more carefully in the essays on the administration of the Sacrament of Penance and on Spiritual Direction. It is right to dwell here upon the fact that some experienced priests spend much time in clearing up the troubles which flow from wrong and mistaken advice given by others.

This wrong kind of direction is almost always the result of ignorance. Priests who are not sufficiently instructed for so great a responsibility are called upon to fulfil it. Nowadays the duty of hearing confessions comes to far more priests than it did only a few years ago. There has been an enormous increase in the number of men, women, and children who use the Sacrament of Penance. Many Evangelicals feel bound to admit the necessity, in some cases at least, for the making of a confession. They realize also that the clergy should be competent to give such advice as is necessary. If this is so general, then it follows that the most careful training must be given, not to a few special priests, but to all.

It is sometimes suggested that the bishops should appoint and train certain men for the duty of hearing confessions. I cannot think that any parish priest who understands his office would permit, save in exceptional circumstances, a peripatetic stranger to come round regularly to hear his people's confessions. Indeed, this was one of the chief causes of dispute between secular and religious clergy in the Middle Ages. No, the right confessors for a parish are the parish priest and his assistants—if he has them. But it is absurd to suppose that a generally religious life, combined with common sense and the reading of the plays of Shakespeare and good novels (as was once suggested to me), will qualify a man for the effective discharge of so technical a work as spiritual direction.

At any moment in any confession a matter may arise which calls for special knowledge. It may, for instance, affect the penitent's relation to the law of the land, or to a moral law of the Church, matters which require far more than common sense for their solution. It is necessary, in fact, that a confessor should be closely acquainted with that technical branch of learning known as moral theology. The Church has for centuries been working it out, and it is now fairly clear, ascertainable, and coherent.

One qualification, however, may be made here. Only a few years ago there were very few books on moral theology written by priests of the Church of England. We were therefore thrown back to a great extent on Roman Catholic books. These are, in themselves, admirable, but they need adaptation if they are to be safely used by those who have to deal with members of the Church of England. It must be remembered that these books presuppose compulsory confession—at least at Easter. In many ways, therefore, they need cautious application in the Church of England whose formularies do not contemplate obligatory confession.

In any case, profound and careful study of moral theology is necessary for all Anglican priests. This should begin at the theological college, but should continue throughout the priestly life. There are now a good many sound books on moral theology by Anglicans, and more are in preparation. The reading of these books must go side by side with practical experience ; but there is every sign that, as in the last twenty-five years there has been a great increase in the number of penitents, so also the number will go on growing. We must be prepared to meet the demand efficiently.

I do not wish to trespass on ground which will be occupied by other writers in this book. This particular essay is of the nature of a general introduction, and I felt it might be as well to clear the ground a little in order to

make way for others. These are critical days
of change and development. In particular, the
more specifically Catholic penitential method is
only gradually being worked out among us.
It is to be wished that our bishops may themselves take in hand such matters as are dealt
with here.

The policy of the authorities of the Church
has for too long been to allow great movements
to start and get under way, and perhaps make
mistakes ; then either to attempt to arrest
them, or else to take the line of half-ignorant
disapproval. The Anglo-Catholic priest has
been left almost entirely to himself without
guidance or direction from his bishops in some
of the most essential parts of his ministry. The
Anglo-Catholic movement itself is still regarded
as sectional, partisan, and negligible. The
Church of England must decide, so it seems to
me, whether she is going to use, or not to use,
the immense force which is now actually being
exercised by Anglo-Catholic priests everywhere. It is surely time that the Church of
England determined to harness and use this
power. If this is a digression, it comes out of
the consideration of the life and work of the
priest in the Church of England to-day.

The Equipment of the Modern Priest

In writing of the equipment of the clergy
for their work in these modern days, I want to

deal with one matter which may be regarded as a small one, but which cuts deeper than is commonly recognized. I mean their mode of dressing. I know all there is to be said for dressing like a layman. I have heard many times about the importance of meeting men on their own ground, and I am told of the advantage of not frightening them by the wearing of a ' dog collar.' I know people are supposed to give their confidence more quickly to a man they do not suspect of being a parson than to one who is dressed as a priest. I distrust all these arguments, and especially the last one. Indeed, I do not believe in these methods. I hope I am not narrow about it. I see no particular reason for climbing the Matterhorn or even Skiddaw, or for walking on Scottish moors, in a clerical collar ; but I do believe people should know when they are in the company of a priest ; and therefore I think it is fair to himself and the laity that even on a holiday abroad the priest should dress as one—at least in the evening. Anyway, I do not think the quasi-layman method achieves its purpose, at least with men worth talking to. It is seldom even a successful disguise. A soft collar and a black or grey tie, united—so says the enemy—with a certain cast of countenance, is as unmistakably clerical attire to-day as an all-round collar and a long black coat.

If a priest knows his business, if he is the kind of man other men will trust, they will be

just as ready to talk to him if he wears priestly
dress as if he is clothed in a lovely brown suit
with a Royal Stuart tartan tie. While if he is
not the kind of man they trust, no glory of
costume will gain their confidence. Even supposing it were so, is it fair to entrap an unhappy
layman into conversation under false pretences ?
It is not unlikely he may be seriously annoyed
when he finds out, as he probably will in the
end, that he has been tricked. Most men are
just as ready to tell a parson what they think
about parsons, and other subjects, as to tell
a layman the same things, provided always he
is the right sort of parson.

Seriously, I am sure that what the best kind
of man is wanting to-day in a priest is one who
really understands his job, and neither is, or
pretends to be, a layman nor an amateur. The
word ' professional ' in this sense has rather a
sinister sound, but using the word rightly that
is what I mean. Every other professional man
is rightly expected to be competent in his own
department—certainly he is not ashamed of his
profession. If he is it is not likely he will be a
success in it. Why should the clergy alone
be unprofessional ? Why should they pretend
to be something other than what they are ?
After all, the priesthood is the noblest of all
professions—at any rate in our estimation.
What does it matter if in some ages of history,
and in some parts of the world to-day, priests
have made bad use of the power entrusted to

them ? We deplore the fact, and are warned. It will take a long time to clear away this reproach altogether; but, on the other hand, we of the clergy in England, and especially, I believe, we who are Anglo-Catholics, have a splendid opportunity of setting forth a renewed ideal of priesthood in these modern days. We have been ready enough to deplore the breach of the Catholic tradition in England. It is well to remember that the breach has not been altogether without its advantages. At any rate it has provided us with a fresh field for thought and practice.

Theological Knowledge

Now let us consider briefly one or two other necessary parts of the equipment of the priestly profession. The Church of England has passed through strange stages, but few have been so remarkable as that in which mistrust and contempt were felt for technical theological knowledge. During the last fifty years the study of theology had fallen into low estimation, especially at the Universities. It used to be considered that a man who had taken a degree at Oxford or Cambridge was fully qualified for Ordination, though he might have read practically no theology at all. Even I can remember the days when the Honour School of Theology at Oxford was considered as easily the last and least important of all. That, happily, is changed now. The science of the knowledge of God,

c

though still too often regarded for some in-
scrutable reason as of secondary importance, is
at any rate considered indispensable for the
equipment of a priest.

Few of us can ever be scholars in the strictly
technical sense.   The innumerable and necessary activities of the parish priest of to-day, at
any rate in cities, make that impossible ; but
the training of the younger generation of priests
is very different from that of their elders.
The reinstatement of theological study in something like its right place at the Universities
is already bringing forth good results.   In
the future, the Church of England will have
a more learned clergy than in the past.   The
bishops are wisely insisting upon a much
higher standard : a fact which is likely to
be of great moment in that revival of religion
which some of us are optimistic enough to
expect.

This consideration carries with it the further
corollary hinted at above, that theological
students must be aware of modern tendencies
and modern views of religion.   Indeed this
battle may be said to be won.   But the word
modernist is a question-begging one, and
should either be more carefully defined or
used more sparingly.   Yet while some clergy
are still rather suspicious of the up-to-date
theology at Oxford and Cambridge, the old
order has passed.   It may be objected that
this is all rather vague.   What does it all

mean ? I will make matters clearer by giving one instance.

The reception of the volume called *Essays Catholic and Critical* by Anglo-Catholics in general, and by their press in particular, was a portentous sign of the times. Only ten or twelve years ago I believe it would have met with a strong, vigorous, and quite widespread opposition. The way in which it has, in fact, been received is not yet seen in all its importance. But at least one parrot cry has been strangled. We were constantly assured until a short time ago that Anglo-Catholics were perhaps pious, but certainly mostly fools, who had no reputable scholars among them. We are now told, on very high authority, that Anglo-Catholics have more than their fair share of the brains of the Church of England. What has happened surely means that a great change is coming over the mental equipment of the English priesthood.

THE INTERIOR LIFE

If it is important that the modern priest should be sufficiently learned, and enough of a theologian to be professionally equipped for his work in these difficult days, it is at least as important that his theology should be based on an interior life of prayer. I purpose to conclude this essay with a brief reference to the priest's prayers. I do so in a spirit of the deepest humility, and with the utmost penitence for innumerable personal failures. God forbid that I should dare to instruct or to judge others. Yet experience leads me to plead with all my power for an ordered and disciplined priestly life governed by strict Rule. This particularly applies not only to priests who are cloistered, but to those who are living in the world. The spiritual life can never in its essence depend upon times of feeling and impulse, but must in the last resort rest upon discipline. God may give, or may withdraw, what is called ' sensible devotion '—this is neither our business nor our responsibility. Our duty is to be always ready for the divine Visitor ; to be always ' breaking up our fallow ground ' for the descent of God's blessing upon it : and that means Rule.

I have found throughout my own priestly life that it is an untold help to be a member of one of those societies of priests which bind together their members by a common Rule of Life. I find that my experience is shared in this respect by many of the priests whose example I most desire to follow. There are several such societies of priests, and their Rules do not materially differ. The advantages of membership are many. In the first place, a priest's Rule of Life is not merely his own individual choice. Outside the obedience to which the Church binds us all, as a member of a society he shares its Rule with others ; he has the support of knowing that fifty, sixty, or a hundred priests, many of whom are his personal

friends, are sharing his spiritual Rule with him.
He meets them from time to time. He reports
progress to the Superior. He knows that if
he gets slack in any part of his Rule he does not
merely fail for himself but weakens the whole
body to which he belongs. He knows that so
far as he is faithful he upholds many others
beside himself. In both ways the corporate
sense helps. Man is weak, and many a priest
would admit his fears that he might have grown
slack about this or that part of the inner life
had he not been supported by the obligation of
his Rule.

In outline, of course, the basis of such
societies corresponds with the universal obligations of the priesthood, carried further in some
details. It will include, for instance, the Rule
of celebrating, or at least being present at, Mass
daily—one day in the week being sometimes
excepted. Even if it be not stated in the Rule,
careful preparation for and thanksgiving after
Mass will be taken for granted, together with
the most scrupulous punctuality in the time of
beginning the service.

The recitation of the Divine Office of Morning and Evening Prayer is, as we all know, an
obligation on priests of the Church of England,
and in the spirit expressed in the preface to
another great office book of the Church :
' reverently, attentively, and with devotion.'
But what a world of difference there can be in
our manner of saying Morning and Evening

Prayer ! It may mean everything or nothing. Most of us know what a help it is to have an ' intention ' when saying the Office—some person, some cause, some idea in our mind. When we say our Office in this manner the words take a new meaning, new light breaks out of the old and shines back upon the old.

Further, all the societies of which I have knowledge make confession to a priest one of their obligations. This is no doubt something over and above what the Church of England absolutely requires even from its ministers ; but, apart from all other considerations, it is difficult to understand how a man who may at any moment be called upon to hear a confession can avoid making his own ; while the priest, perhaps more than any one else, feels the continual need of spiritual direction in his own life. In the nature of things he must have temptations and perplexities which do not come within the experience of the laity. He who has great responsibilities towards others needs great assistance himself.

A Rule for the practice of meditation is also, I believe, common to Anglo-Catholic societies of priests. It has usually been found necessary to make it perfectly strict as to time—at least as to a minimum time each week ; for meditation on the mysteries of God must not depend upon an impulse, nor on moments of spiritual elevation. If it did, some would be poorly off. But, as many of us believe, meditation

must be part of a fixed Rule.   Time must be
set apart, fenced off for it, and we must go to it
whether we happen to be inclined or disinclined.
There is no need, for I write unto wise men, to
say anything of the joy and progress which
come from regular and disciplined meditation.

Other Rules are sometimes added bearing
on simplicity of life, careful spending of money,
and avoidance of extravagance or too great
luxury.   All these are helpful.

These are the fountains of the priestly interior
life as it has been historically understood in
Catholic tradition.   It is but a beginning, a
necessary starting-point which is meant in the
end to lead to eternal union with and love of
God.   It is this fact which frees it from any
suspicion of formality.   It cannot be suggested
that it is a Rule with which the priest will be
satisfied.   On the contrary, it is but the starting-
point in the adventure of eternity.

I know that many priests who belong to no
society other than the Church are living lives
as holy and disciplined as any can be.   I only
write of this kind of Rule because of the help
which in my experience it has brought to
priests young and old.   At any rate we are
all agreed upon one point, whatever may be
our priestly activity, or whatever our ecclesiastical office or school of thought : we unite in
the necessity of living an interior life in which
we seek one thing and one only—growing
union with God.   It is only in so far as we

possess this hidden castle of the soul that we are able to go out to the perplexities and responsibilities which of necessity belong to the priestly life. 'The man of God must be perfect, throughly furnished unto all good works.'

INTELLECTUAL PROBLEMS

By Edward Gordon Selwyn

II

INTELLECTUAL PROBLEMS

Some Governing Considerations

'MY duty towards God, is to believe in
him, to fear him, and to love him
with all my heart, *with all my mind*. . . .'
And this teaching of Christ is echoed by His
Apostles ; as when S. Paul in his later Epistles
dwells upon knowledge as the ripe fruit of
faith, or S. Peter insists on the Christians'
readiness to answer those who ask them the
reason of their hope. It means that man's
intellect has a worship to offer for which neither
his will nor his feeling can stand proxy. That
is why teaching has always lain at the very heart
of the Church's pastoral work. It was so with
our Lord, most of whose recorded utterances
are of the nature of teaching rather than of
preaching, and addressed to His disciples rather
than indiscriminately to crowds. Clement with
his classes at Alexandria and S. Cyril with his
catechetical lectures at Jerusalem were making
no innovation in the Church's practice, but con-
tinuing and adapting a tradition which derived
without break from Christ Himself. The
beautiful rites and ceremonies connected with

Christian initiation[1] in the early centuries attest the same principle, and show how the illumination of the mind was reckoned indispensable to membership of the Church. At a much later date, again, when the mind of Europe was awakening from the confused sleep of the Dark Ages, it was the main purpose of Aquinas and the scholastic writers to give a new precision to Christian thought and thus equip it to hold its own in an age of intellectual renaissance. A like aim animated the great Anglican divines of the seventeenth and eighteenth centuries ;— men like Beilby Porteous, Bishop of Chester, and women like Hannah More, the pioneers of our Sunday Schools, and the great doctrinal teachers of the Oxford Movement. It may safely be said, indeed—and it is one of the characteristic marks of Catholic Christianity—that every great revival has taken the form of a new interest in, and care for, the great province of teaching.

It needs but little reflection upon the modern world to see why this principle of the Church's life and witness is to-day more important than ever. Up to a hundred years ago the Church held the keys of knowledge. It was not always perhaps a good steward; but, broadly speaking, little was done for education which it did not at once promote and carry through ; and a

---

[1] I adopt the term from the Rev. N. P. Williams's essay in *Essays Catholic and Critical* as covering Baptism, Confirmation, and Penance.

host of Universities and Colleges, of Public Schools and elementary schools, bears witness to its zeal for the cause of knowledge. But this very fact of being alone, or at any rate first, in the field gave it an immense hold upon the whole intellectual life of society : so that the problems which chiefly confronted men were largely of the Church's setting, and their answers at least suggested out of Christian books and teaching.

To-day a variety of causes—chief of which is the vast increase of population in Western Europe—has conspired to effect material change in this situation. It is true that the Church is still, particularly in our own country, in the thick of national education ; and it is arguable that few intellectual problems become living issues for any large section of people, unless religion, either by encouragement or by re-action, brings them to the forefront of interest. Darwinism would hardly have had the vogue it had, if Huxley had had no bishops to break lances with ; nor would anthropology have advanced so quickly, had not Christian missions brought home the importance of understanding the tribal lore of those whom they sought to evangelize. But, when all this is said, the last century has confronted the Church with a changed situation. In civilized countries to-day we have to deal with whole peoples who are educated, and whose education has been largely independent of the Church's direct in-

fluence. Not only is reading universal; but
every industry and avocation has its supply of
technical journals, which bring morsels of
contemporary science, art, and economics to
the mind's door; while an eager Press trans-
mits ideas with lightning rapidity from one
end of the globe to the other.

In such an atmosphere the old distinction
between the *ecclesia docens* and the *ecclesia
discens* loses much of its force. In old days the
Church provided the nation both with teachers
and learners ; and the one section taught, and
the other learned from it, all subjects alike.
But both those conditions have ceased to operate
now. State and municipality have become independent educational authorities, with their own
traditions of intellectual interest and attention ;
while the growing complexity of knowledge
has compelled both teachers and learners to
specialize. Specialization is, indeed, the dominating fact of modern life and knowledge.
History and philosophy, the two great hand-
maidens of Christian theology, are now approached, if at all, along a multitude of avenues
by those who sit in our pews; and in the Church,
as in society at large, a subtly articulated
democracy of knowledge has taken the place of
the old relationship between the priest and his
people. Even in sacred learning, which is the
peculiar province and duty of the priest, he no
longer has a monopoly ; for he may well find
members of his congregation who have read

widely and thought deeply in this sphere. The Church's accredited minister has, no doubt, something peculiar to contribute, and to this we shall come in a moment : but others also have their contribution to make, and it is only in the spirit of co-operation that the intellectual office of the pastorate can be accomplished.

If this is a situation which presents many problems, it is also one full of promise and hope. It means a greatly increased sensitiveness, throughout the whole spiritual body, to the intellectual implications of the Faith. It is often said that the result of this is to make men turn away from any authoritative teaching of religion, and to discredit dogma. But, in so far as that is true, it is true of the shallower minds, not of the deeper. The effect on more thoughtful natures is of a different kind. It is to discredit, not dogma, but dogmatism, and to lead men not so much to turn away from authority as to seek to understand its credentials. Men are well aware that they constantly resort to authority, and are justified in doing so, for guidance in matters of secular knowledge and conduct : what they want to be assured of is that *in sacris* the appeal to authority has equally good grounds in reason and common sense. And the kind of authority so required is clearly one that will stimulate thought, not stifle it ; and, in saying what is true, will open the way to the pursuit of fresh truth and illuminate still more of those subtle links and ligaments of knowledge which are our guarantee that the kingdom of Truth is one.

It is in this spirit that men look to the priest to help them to make sense of their own lives and of the life of society around them ; just as they look to the man of science to make sense of the physical universe, and to the artist to make sense of the beauty whose fugitive forms cross and re-cross the walks of our experience. And when they are so helped and guided, then they are stronger witnesses to Christ and better equipped for the warfare of His Church than was possible when education was the privilege of the few.

CONSEQUENT REQUIREMENTS IN THE MINISTRY

What, then, are the qualities of priest-craft called for by this fact of universal education ? For better or worse, it is not disputable that in the functioning of religious institutions the personality of the ministry is of vital importance. Rightly or wrongly men's impression of the Church and its claims is intimately connected with the impression they form of its accredited ministers. The clergy cannot help being focal points in that highly-charged field of spiritual tendencies and forces which is embodied as the Church ; and the question is how they are to discharge their office worthily and well.

One answer we may dismiss at once. It is

not possible, nor is it desirable, that the priest should seek to be, or to appear to be, at home in every branch of knowledge represented among those to whom he ministers. That would be to forget the fact already mentioned that specialization is the dominant characteristic of modern society and its mental life. There is an old saying that we only begin to be educated when we begin to discover our ignorance; and there is no one who needs to remember it more than the priest. He must, of course, now more than ever, be himself well educated; but that is not to say that he must covet a smattering of every subject. The result could only be disastrous—disastrous to his work, for superficial knowledge is soon exposed, and even more disastrous to himself in the growth of a distracted, and therefore a spiritually infertile, mind.

There are, however, certain qualities, tempers, and habits of mind which it is safe to say are specially needed for pastoral work to-day ; and it may be well to try to enumerate some of them.

(*a*) First of all I should place a certain attitude towards truth, both as it is in itself and to the discipline of its discovery. Here is common ground between all who can be said to cultivate in any sense an intellectual life. Yet it is not obviously common : and the Church has perhaps few more important tasks than to make it plain. To say that modern knowledge

D

is specialized is to say that it is centrifugal. Men and women spend their working days in the pursuit of countless avocations, each of which has its own technique ; and it is only in the more advanced stages that these various walks of life and thought can be seen to inter-lace and have a common origin and common end. The truths and principles proper to each appear for the most part self-sufficient and adequate ; and the mind easily comes to be content with them, and to think that there is no truth of importance outside its own beat ; or else, if it does feel ambitious, to suppose that the categories it is accustomed to work with will, if pressed far enough, serve to interpret the whole field of reality.

The first of these conditions is responsible for much that is ascribed to-day to indifference or even to materialism ; the second for the much rarer phenomenon of self-conscious unbelief. Yet both are really products of specialization : they belong to the rut. And it is just here that the Church can perform a very valuable and very welcome service, by its wit-ness to the larger and more comprehensive truth of which these other truths are parts. The service is welcome, because the mind, even in its rut, is really pregnant with intimations of that larger field of truth and knowledge which lies outside it ; and its discovery brings all the relief which comes to a mother after travail. Moreover, none is so well trained for the midwife's task as the Church. For its foundation-faith is a belief in one God, who is Creator, Lord, and End of all, in whom we live and move and have our being. It sees in Christ the eternal Son incarnate in whom all things have their coherence. It acknowledges and partakes of one Holy Spirit of wisdom, sweetly ordering all things and giving to each individual task or truth its meaning and place in the whole. And the priest's office is to present God in this comprehensiveness of power and sympathy : not as the great Individual over against earth's puny individuals, but as the great Universal in whom all particulars of life and truth are gathered up.

(*b*) If this witness is to be effectively borne, it will require in the ministry some knowledge both of philosophy and of history ; for philosophy and history are the two paths along which natural knowledge advances furthest to meet that knowledge of God which comes through revelation, and in which the blending of the two processes—man's discovery and God's self-disclosure—is most clearly seen. Both studies, moreover, impose upon the mind a rigorous discipline, if they are to yield their proper fruit ; and the exercise of this discipline is of even greater importance than the range of ground which is covered. To have a thorough acquaintance of some one problem of philosophy or some one period of history, to have mastered the principles of criticism which each elicits and illustrates, to have learnt to see all the facts and not only the convenient ones, and to weigh probabilities fairly before reaching a conclusion—this is indispensable for a mind that is to give confidence to others.

And that is the first requisite in the priest to-day—that he should give confidence. Men want to know not that the priest can answer their questions, but that he knows how they ought to be approached, or (it may be) how they can be better asked. His own dogmatic and moral teaching, moreover, will gain everything when it is seen against a background of solid and reliable thinking. Over and over again it is the background of what we say, and not its direct content, which leaves the enduring mark. For it is the background which is the common ground; and the priest must win the confidence of his people there, if they are to go on with him, as he must hope that they will, to be fully instructed members of Christ's Church.

(*c*) The priest, then, must possess the conviction, derived from his belief in God, that Truth is one ; and he must show that those truths which are especially his to teach have been won and assimilated by him at the cost of the same scrupulous fidelity to facts and laborious attention to detail as are exacted by the quest of truth in every other walk of life. But there is yet a third and crowning quality which is needed. If he is to help others to make sense of their own lives, it must be evident that he has learnt how to make sense of his own. In other words, there is nothing which makes a stronger intellectual reaction than holiness.

It seems a paradox to say that true liberty of mind is only found where every thought is brought into captivity to Christ ; and yet it is profoundly and vitally true. No mind impresses us more forcibly than one which has been accustomed to take all its problems ' into the sanctuary of God.' The reason is that what we are seeking in all problems of faith and doubt is not so much the answer to a question as the response to a need. The desire for truth is in itself the desire of the intellect for love : and the life governed by love for God is the most convincing of all testimonies that the truth can be found. The late Bishop Paget of Oxford has a memorable passage upon this point :

It was to make known to us the law of liberty, to write it in our hearts, to make it paramount over the activities alike of intellect and will, that the Holy Spirit came to dwell in men.

Yes ; if we would know more of intellectual liberty, let us see whether it is not really to be gained by simply and humbly bringing our lives into more constant and more thankful submission to His guidance, to His enlightening and renewing Presence. For is not this a part of His work ? Through the ministry of grace and truth He makes known to men the love of God, shown forth in Jesus Christ our Lord ; and as the astounding tenderness and glory of that love begins to dawn upon them, He stirs in them some sense of what might be the joy and strength and peace of a human life that was filled with such a love as that ; and then He bears into their hearts the hope that, for Christ's sake, that life, if they will have it, will even yet be theirs. And in proportion as that hope grows real and pure and clear within them, they begin with single-mindedness to look towards God and to live as in His sight ; and so the things of this world—its praise, its prizes, its contentions, its prejudices—loose their hold upon the mind, and a new sense of strength and independence comes to it, as it begins to see even afar off its rest for ever in the truth of God.[1]

Types of Intellectual Difficulty

If it be the case that the pastorate of the mind calls not so much for answers to questions as for response to needs, it means that the Church's approach to the intellectual difficulties and problems of its members is not made solely, or even mainly, on academic lines. Its manner of handling them is at once less subtle and more profound—less subtle, because it knows that dialectic in inexpert hands often becomes little more than sophistry ; and deeper, because it never detaches the problem from the person who is wrestling with it.

Here, too, there is a question of background; and the priest's business, in seeking to help those who are puzzled, is to try to reach the background of the perplexity. The intellectual difficulties of University students no doubt present special conditions which are not normally found in later life ; but even here, though

[1] *The Spirit of Discipline*, pp. 108–9 (Sermon on ' Freedom of Thought ').

the currency of the discussion bears more
obviously the stamp of the academic mint, the
problems at issue commonly run up into the
disposition and growth of the whole personality.
It is in that hidden shrine of the individual soul
that the problems are for the most part set.
All the influences which have gone to the soul's
shaping—those of home, of school, of friends,
its temptations and its triumphs, its moments
of vivid experience and of quiet reflection—all
these are twined around the roots of the mind's
criticism, inquiry, or doubt, and give to them
their background. And it is the condition
represented by this background which needs
diagnosis.

Broadly speaking, I think we may distin-
guish four main types of intellectual difficulty
as likely to meet the priest in his work and to
call for his sympathy and skill.

(*a*) *Difficulties due to lack of teaching*. It
is probably impossible to exaggerate the wide
potency of this cause. It is indeed the inevitable result of an educational system which
the Church touches only at certain points.
There are large sections of all classes of our
population to-day which are wholly ignorant
alike of the historical facts on which the Chris-
tain faith is based, of the revelation of God
which they involve, and of the meaning of any
act of worship. The private schoolboy who
had never heard of the Crucifixion, the Army
officer who asked whether the use of water in

Baptism was not 'a new idea,' the artist who could not believe that God was an old man with a white beard [1]—these are instances, even if perhaps extreme, of a condition all too widespread.

In cases of this kind, the intellectual difficulties presented are often not of a very stubborn kind. The springs of character may quite well be pure, and the mind virgin soil ; and the problem is one of simple and straightforward instruction. This may be given individually or in classes ; but probably the most powerful incentive to the learner will come through membership in the worshipping body. Religion must be caught as well as taught. There was an important principle enunciated in Pascal's celebrated maxim, ' Begin by taking holy water, and you will end by believing the Catholic Faith.' To take a part, however humble, in a ceremony, however simple, is to find oneself the member of a body, and to be forced to ask questions about it. 'What mean ye by this service ? ' was a good beginning for the Jewish child's knowledge of God and of His ways, and it serves the Christian too. It is of the essence of ceremony that it fixes the attention, and of religious ceremony that it fixes it in reverence ; and reverent attention is the best state of mind that can be induced as a preparation for imparting the truths of God.

[1] All these three cases have been brought to the present writer's notice within the last few years.

There are, of course, cases where the problem is more difficult than this. The mind is never a *tabula rasa*, and one who has learnt no religious faith may yet have contracted deep religious prejudices. Of these it may be said that it is rarely any use to try to deal with them direct ; they are in their nature irrational, and need to be forgotten rather than renounced. Patient friendship will be the best help here, combined with a kindly forbearance for what theologians have called ' invincible ignorance.'[1]

(*b*) *Difficulties due to misunderstanding of Scripture.* These are very common, and are found among people of the most diverse intellectual calibre. They range from the insuperable obstacle to believing in Christ which was felt by Henry Sidgwick, on the ground of the non-fulfilment of our Lord's eschatological predictions, to the loss of faith which so often follows upon unanswered prayer. It might seem strange to class these two types of problem together : but they have in fact the same root ; for both alike spring from the attempt to understand Scripture without reference to the Church which is its background. In such cases particular texts or passages of Scripture become isolated from their true context, and present difficulties which, when once this isolation is effected, are probably quite insoluble.

[1] This condition is the subject of an interesting discussion by the Rev. K. E. Kirk in *Ignorance, Faith, and Conformity* (Longmans, 1925).

The problem, for example, with which Henry Sidgwick wrestled—that of our Lord's eschatological teaching—is one that simply as a matter of historical or literary criticism may be said to be still unsolved : but it is one that only becomes acute for faith, when the basis of faith is supposed to be the literal interpretation of our Lord's words. Yet that is to use as the basis of faith a principle which none accept as the basis of conduct. With regard to our Lord's ethical teaching, we freely admit that it must be interpreted in the spirit rather than the letter, and that we must go behind the recorded word to the whole context of events and ideas lying behind it, if we are to discern its truth aright. The same is true of His apocalyptic teaching : we have no right to ascribe to our Lord a literalness there which we disown elsewhere ; and when His predictions of the establishment of the kingdom are brought into connection with that mighty outpouring of grace and power which was seen in the Resurrection and the foundation of the Church, and is still experienced in the work of the Holy Spirit, they become rather aids than obstacles to belief in the Incarnation.

A like principle holds good in the case of unanswered prayer. ' I prayed that God would spare that beloved life, and it has been taken from me ; how can I believe in Him or pray to Him any longer ? '—there are thousands who have given up the practice of prayer on such a ground. Yet it may be questioned whether the problem would ever reach this degree of acuteness, if it were not for certain recorded utterances of Christ, which seem to make the unconditional promise that petitions made in faith will be unanswered.

Certainly there is nothing in our Lord's revelation of the Father as a whole which would lead us to suppose that whatever we asked for we should literally receive. He teaches us that human fatherhood is a true analogue, so far as it goes, of the divine ; and we do not reckon it a part of a good father to give his children all that they ask. His aim is not to gratify them but to train and educate them ; and in the fulfilment of that end he must often say them nay. He has others, too, it may be, to think of, and in the interests of the younger or the weaker may have to require some sacrifice of the elder or the stronger. So is it, the Christian believes, with God, who spared not His own Son, though there fell from Him as He prayed in Gethsemane ' as it were great drops of blood.'

The Cross, which is at the heart of the Catholic religion, is the great example of un-answered prayer ; and it is to that supreme revelation of God that all other unanswered prayer must be referred. Nor is our Lord's teaching about prayer, *if taken as a whole*, at variance with this. The prayer He promises to answer is prayer offered in His Name—

prayer offered, that is to say, in the spirit of His own complete obedience as Son. And such prayer is always answered, if not by the granting of our petition, yet by the angel strengthening us with grace from heaven.

In all such cases where intellectual difficulty is caused or accentuated by passages of Scripture, the doubting mind needs to be recalled to the background of the living Church out of which the Scriptures arose and to which they were given. There is hardly a difficulty men feel to-day which has not been felt over and over again in the long story of the Church's life ; and what it could not solve it could at least outlive.

Two cautions, however, need constantly to be borne in mind. One is that difficulties of this kind are as often as not of the Church's own making, the result of defective or even definitely erroneous teaching. The other is that there are many problems of biblical interpretation to which no satisfactory solution has yet been given ; and the priest must be ready to admit it. But that, after all, is not to lower the value of Scripture, but to exalt it, for the reverent mind. For it is to claim that the revelation there contained is still in large measure unexplored, and still sufficient therefore for every doubter as well as for every believer, provided that with industry, humility, and hope he will set about the task of inquiry.

(c) *Difficulties due to heretical teaching.* Not

all false teaching is heretical ; for it may be due
to no more than a sincere, but mistaken, attempt
to represent the faith and mind of the Church.
Both reactionary and modernist teaching might
in this sense be false ; but they would not
necessarily be heretical.   Heresy, as the deri-
vation of the word suggests, always implies an
element of wilfulness, and is properly used only
of teaching which definitely sets itself up as
superior to the faith and mind of the Church.
Great dangers attach to merely mistaken teaching ; but when it is given in good faith, the
integrity of the intention is commonly of more
abiding influence than the error involved in its
accomplishment.   In the case of heresy, on
the other hand, the moral contagion of pride
and self-will is never dissociable from the teaching, and bears the disastrous fruits of sectarian-
ism and schism.

The commonest source of heresy to-day is
what it was in the first ages of the Church's
history—the belief that what is outward, material, and social cannot be spiritual.   The hydra-
headed body of thought which appears now as
Theosophy,[1] now as Spiritualism, now as Christian Science, is essentially at one with Gnosticism in this.   Matter is evil or unreal or both,
and the true aim of religion is to detach the
mind from anything so concrete as history or

[1] An admirable account of this will be found in a little
book called *Theosophy* by the late Sister Rhoda (Miss E. R.
McNeile), who was drowned in the S.S. *Egypt*.

so definite as dogma. On this view there is
clearly no room for the belief that the world is
God's creation, or that He became incarnate in
it in human flesh, or that He instituted the
Church to be His visible body and the Sacraments to be means of grace. That whole *corpus*
of teaching which is built on and around the
Incarnation is rejected as crude and carnal ;
and its place is taken by a series of divers
speculations which purport to set the relation
between God and man on a more 'spiritual'
basis.

The convinced votary of any of these modern
forms of Gnosticism is no easier to convert than
his forbear of eighteen centuries ago ; but there
are many who are not convinced, but only as
yet toying with the ideas, and certain considerations may well be pressed with vigour upon
such persons.

There is first the fact—often more discon-
certing than any other kind of argument—
that these ideas are not new. The attraction
of heresy is often little more than its claim to be
modern and up to date ; and to disprove the
claim is often to dispel the attraction. To do
this successfully the priest needs to have some
first-hand knowledge of the controversies of the
second and third centuries, and to remember
that the issues, though the Church has defined
its mind in regard to them, are still real for
many people.

Secondly, we need to emphasize the unique

and complete sufficiency of the mediation of Christ and of His Spirit. All these cults fall foul in one way or another of this central conception of Christianity, that Christ is the touchstone, and His Spirit the means, of all true intercourse between God and man. We are not concerned, any more than was S. John, to deny the variety of real spiritual influences which play upon the soul of man ; nor shall we regard death as setting an inexorable limit to the potentialities of this ' communion of saints.' But we shall insist that all such secondary mediation is grounded in, and subsidiary to, and always to be tested by, that one sovereign mediation which is given in the Person of Christ. ' To confess that Jesus the anointed is come in the flesh . . . is to confess that there is one Mediator for all men ' : [1] and to supersede or to overlay this mediation with others which are independent of it is to be in league with the ' spirit of antichrist.'

And, thirdly, we shall do well to point to the inevitably anti-social tendency of all those beliefs which begin by disesteeming the material, the historical, the visible. They represent a kind of Pharisaism of the intellect, for which the common life of humanity is something in itself unclean. True religion, on this view, consists not in following Christ's example and taking the burden of man's nature more and

[1] F. D. Maurice, *The Epistles of S. John*, Lecture xiv. The whole of this powerful lecture should be consulted.

more upon us, but in an escape from that reality into a world of private and privileged emancipation. The lump of mankind, compact of great physical and economic relationships, is not to be leavened, but to be shunned: its sins and sorrows are to be cozened away as unreal, its blindnesses abandoned for the dark lanterns of sorcery, its theologies refined away into the mists of speculation. And to argue and act so is anti-social. You cannot help men that way.

It is no matter for surprise that these cults should have never yet succeeded in leaving any abiding mark upon those durable social structures—the village, the town, the school, the nation—which are the makers and subjects of history. For the leavening of those lumps there is needed not a coterie, but a Church ; not a séance, but a Sacrament. And Church and Sacrament are only found where the faith of the Incarnation has been accepted and lived as the hallowing of all social relationships.

(*d*) *Difficulties due to the parsimony of revelation*. I have chosen this phrase to describe those ultimate philosophical difficulties which beset all religious belief,[1] because it indicates what I conceive to be characteristic of the Christian attitude towards them. They are felt by different minds in very varying degree, and more by those of philosophical and intro-

---

[1] If I had to name any one book upon these problems, it would be *Faith and Truth* by the Revs. F. H. Brabant and Percy Hartill.

spective temperament than by men of action.
But they are in themselves far more impersonal,
more intrinsic to religion, and therefore more
universal, than any of those which we have so
far considered.

To name such cardinal elements of all faith
as God, Freedom, Immortality, is to call up
from the vasty deep of our experience of life
a multitude of facts which seem to say them
nay. How, in face of pain, can God be love ?
How in a world of natural law can man alone
claim freedom ? What but the sanguineness
of his hope should give him ground to think
himself immortal ?

It need hardly be said that the attempt to
suggest answers to these questions would fall
outside the scope of this essay. But there
are certain practical aspects of them which are
closely germane to the pastoral work of the
ministry, and may well be considered here before this chapter is concluded. The first concerns the spirit of our teaching. I have spoken
above of the parsimony of revelation ; and it
is there, I would urge, that the clue to this spirit
lies. In other words, we need to remember
at once how few and how pregnant are those
truths about Himself and His dealings with the
world and with man which it has pleased God
to reveal ; how limited, in consequence, is the
number of the Church's authoritative defini-
tions ; how vast the field of mystery around our
life and thought.

E

There is no deadlier enemy to the presentation of the Faith to thoughtful men and women than that ' concision ' of the mind which offers a cut-and-dried answer to every question and seeks to bring every problem within the ambit of some formulary. We have to recognize, as Dr. Gore has often pointed out, the place of agnosticism as the companion of faith in the mind's quest after God. The Church's dogmas are like those lights by which the ship takes it bearings, as it makes port at night. They do not make the darkness day, nor assuage the storm, nor illuminate the mysteries of the deep. Yet the deep is charted, the rocks and shallows indicated, and the fair way shown; and the lights conspire with the skill and labour of the navigators to ensure that harbour is gained.

The second important aspect of these difficulties is correlative to the first, in that the emphasis by the teacher upon the mystery surrounding even the central and most certain truths of the Catholic Faith provides the mental atmosphere in which the individual may best grapple with his own questionings. This was what Newman meant when he said that ' ten thousand difficulties do not make one doubt.' For doubt is a state of mind which is as far removed from the acknowledgement of mystery as it is from the apprehension of truth. That is the permanent lesson of the Book of Job. There are few ultimate problems of religious belief which Job did not face in his misery. And so long as he was confronted simply with the stark facts of his individual experience, or with the gaunt moralizings on them provided by his friends, no solution of them was in sight. What brought relief to his mind was first of all a new atmosphere—the awakening of wonder before the infinite and grotesque complexity, the mysterious power and beauty, of created things. It was when he felt this atmosphere that his difficulties became, not indeed soluble—none of his questions are answered in the book—but tolerable. ' I have heard of Thee by the hearing of the ear : but now mine eye seeth Thee. Wherefore I abhor myself, and repent in dust and ashes.' Why repent ? it may be asked. It was not that his life had not after all been virtuous. It was because both his belief and his doubts had moved too much in the sphere of calculation ; in both he had forgotten the mystery of life. His mind found health and peace only through an intellectual conversion, in which the primary element was wonder.

Finally, something should be said as to the point at which intellectual difficulties of this kind may be rightly regarded, either on the Church's side or on the individual's, as a bar to communion. The two aspects of the question are not really distinct ; for too much rigidity in the Church is often the cause of an unhealthy scrupulousness in the individual.

But, granted that there must be a wide liberty allowed, there is a wide divergence of principle between the methods advocated to ensure it. Broadly speaking, they may be called the Modernist and the Catholic method respectively.

The Modernist method may be summed up as the policy of re-writing the Creeds, with a view to disencumbering them of articles which are supposed to be historically ill-attested or doctrinally over-elaborated, or even verbally archaic and obscure : and various attempts at such revision have been made in recent years. The real fallacy of this policy is first that it greatly overestimates the adequacy of *any* language to compass the truths of religion, and secondly that it still leaves their fundamental difficulties, disguised as they may be by an artificial simplicity of expression, as intransigent as ever. It is not surprising that many Modernists would like to go a step still further, and have no Creeds at all. But that is frankly to abandon the claim that Christianity is a body of rational truth ; and to suppose that its piety or its ethic will long survive such an admission is simply to indulge in a dream.

The Catholic method, on the other hand, is to abate nothing of the Creeds or other authoritative teaching of the Church, but to insist that individuals differ infinitely in their capacity for apprehending different elements in the whole structure or system of truth which are thus represented. The Faith is the community's faith, forged on the anvil of actual experience and in the furnace of actual issues. And, though the story of its growth is not necessarily closed, it is the result of a development. The Church did not come all at once to the Nicene confession or the Chalcedonian definition ; and though S. Peter might have recognized his own faith in that of Aquinas or of Butler, he did not in fact so express it.

But what was true of the Church as a whole is true also of the individual : he assimilates the Faith gradually, part by part, and with many digressions and delays. What matters is that the mind should be on the road—its intention rather than its achievement. And so long as there is the desire to believe the whole truth of Christ, it may be questioned whether any suspense of judgement on particular articles of the Creed should be held to debar from communion. There is a vocation of criticism as well as of faith, and those who are called to it may well have to work with backs turned to light which others see. Only if there is definite repudiation and denial of what is, beyond a doubt, the Church's authoritative teaching is the bond of fellowship broken and membership in the body foregone.

THE PASTORAL TRAINING OF CHILDREN

By Alban Edmond Claxton

III

THE PASTORAL TRAINING OF CHILDREN

AT the outset of an essay on the Pastoral Training of Children a reminder is perhaps still needed that the work for children must be approached in a spirit of reverence. It is not a work to be undertaken lightly ; but, on the contrary, it needs much prayer and study.

For our Lord Himself has revealed the importance of the child as the type of spirituality. ' He called a little child unto Him, and set him in the midst of them, and said, Verily I say unto you, Except ye be converted, and become as little children, ye shall not enter into the kingdom of heaven. Whosoever therefore shall humble himself as this little child, the same is greatest in the kingdom of heaven.' [1] And what Jesus revealed long ago, modern science is at last discovering to be true. ' The qualities foreshadowed in the child seem to be those which will one day be the most valued possession of the race.' [2]

[1] S. Matt. xviii. 2-4.
[2] Professor A. F. Chamberlain, *The Child : a Study in the Evolution of Man.*

57

The child's personality must be reverenced. There are no two created things alike, and the Holy Spirit has implanted in each child potentialities which are to make that child's special character. The child is not a lump of clay to be moulded into the pattern that the priest, or the parent or the teacher, may consider to be the right one ; still less is he a toy for their amusement, or a wild animal to be controlled by fear, repression, or prohibitions. The child is a personality with a character of his own, which will expand and grow in the atmosphere of unselfish love and holy example; and the child learns by what he sees rather than by what he is told ; and discipline is discipleship, the following of the ideal rather than a rigid attention to duty. And the following of the religious ideal comes naturally to children ; they are already at the outset in love with holy things, often to a greater degree than their elders.

Know ye what it is to be a child ? It is to be something very different from the man of to-day. It is to have a spirit yet streaming from the waters of Baptism. It is to believe in love, to believe in loveliness, to believe in belief; it is to be so little that the elves can reach to whisper in your ear ; it is to turn pumpkins into coaches and mice into horses, lowness into loftiness, and nothing into everything, for each child has its fairy godmother in its own soul; it is to live in a nutshell, and to count yourself the king of infinite space.[1]

Yet when all this has been said the priest has a definite work to do for children. He has

[1] Francis Thompson, *Collected Works*, vol. iii.

authority from our Lord to teach them. ' Feed My lambs ' is His commission, and ' Go ye and teach all nations, baptizing them in the Name of the Father, and of the Son, and of the Holy Ghost ; teaching them to observe all things whatsoever I have commanded you.' But his teaching has to be like that of the Good Shepherd, tender and very patient, and with the maternal instincts of S. Paul : ' My little children, of whom I travail in birth again until Christ be formed in you.'[1]

Now to feed the lambs is to give them the Word of God and the Sacraments ; to make known to children their place in the family of God ; that God is Father in the highest and most beautiful sense of Fatherhood ; that Jesus, God's Son, came to be their Elder Brother, came to know children's lives, their joys and sorrows and fears and temptations, came to take their part against the power of evil ; that He showed them how to be the children of His Father's family by His holy example, and made the following of that example possible by the wonderful gift of the Sacraments. The lambs have to be fed with a knowledge that Blessed Mary is their Mother and the saints and angels their brethren ; they have to be surrounded by such a sense of home-liness and love that they will respond and grow and expand in the delight of prayer and wor-ship and Sacrament.

[1] Gal. iv. 19.

THE HOME

Now the priest's work for his children may be said to begin with the child's home. For the home is the true foundation. As a good home is in itself a good training for the wider life of the nation, so much more is a Catholic home a perfect training for the child's life of service in the kingdom of God. For the sake of his children a priest will always be aiming at the making of Catholic homes. A Catholic home is a faint shadow of the life of the Blessed Trinity, of that perfect oneness in love of the Father, the Son, and the Holy Spirit. For in the earthly home is the trinity of father, mother, and child; the lover and his beloved, and the love of the child that binds those two together. The purpose of the home life, the very work of God, is the bringing of children into the world that they in turn may learn to know and love and serve Him here on earth, and so enjoy Him hereafter for ever in heaven.

A Catholic home is the place of ordered liberty where the child is free to develop the Holy Spirit's gifts. The parents should be encouraged to see that there is a crucifix in the rooms. Holy pictures and a prayer corner in the child's bedroom help to make a right atmosphere. Such details as these are important because they make religion natural from earliest days. No amount of religious training by the priest, or the teacher, can ever make up for the lack of religious training in the home. It is a veritable disaster if at the most impressionable age a child should not have about him the atmosphere of the love of God. The following quotation is written from the school standpoint, but is equally true for the priest :

> If both parents understand their relation to God and seek to live in that understanding, they cannot fail to plant the fear and love of God in the children's minds. On that foundation the schools can build, without it there seems no guarantee that the schools can accomplish their task ; they cannot contend against the evil power of selfishness if this inborn tendency is re-inforced by parental example and encouragement.[1]

THE SCHOOL

In many parishes the schools are the property of the Church, and when such is the case the priest has an inestimable opportunity. For in addition to his right as parish priest to teach in his school, the appointment of the teachers is practically in his hands ; and it is not so much the subjects taught as the personal quality of the teacher that counts in the education of young children. That they should be for many hours of the week under the influence of persons who are themselves filled with the spirit of God is of incalculable value. So whilst the Education Authority rightly requires to be satisfied as to the educational qualifications of the teacher, the priest must

[1] *Copec Report on Education*, chap. i.

see that the choice of the school staff is made
with a primary care for their fitness to educate
the children of God.

The teachers are an important part of the
staff of a parish, especially when they are able
to give their teaching in a setting of Catholic
Faith and Practice. The school itself should
be a place where the religious instinct of
the child will find sympathy, understanding,
and love. Because the teachers are living the
Catholic life, and because they come to their
work from the altar, nothing unworthy of a
Christian will be found in their methods.
Irritability, anger, sarcasm, corporal punishment, repressive measures on the part of the
teacher, are definitely hurtful to the child's
soul, and he will not care for the religion of
those whose practice is contrary to their
profession.

Church schools have one advantage only over
the provided schools, but that advantage is the
very reason of their existence. I mean their
religious atmosphere. If the parish priest cannot staff his school with practising Catholics,
and cannot connect the school with the life
and worship of the Church, he may as well give
up the struggle of maintaining his school.

If the priest has an opportunity to do anything for the children of secondary or high
schools in his parish he would naturally use
it ; sometimes a guild in connection with such
schools is possible.

THE CHURCH

Now the priest's own special work for the children begins more really in the church itself. And the secret of our work for them is to remember that we have to teach religion, not merely to teach about religion. It is to make them familiar with religion in a homely, practical way rather than storing the memory with facts. Systematic provision for training in worship and in the use of prayer and the Sacraments is all important. To this end the parish church must be the home of the children. It must be easy of access, a place of delight where they can be sure of a welcome.

So often the doors of our churches present a difficulty to children, they are heavy and hard to open, and often they only lead to further doors and more difficulties. And once inside who shall say that the children will not find an ogre who chases them forth again, caring, as he does, more for the floors and the pews than for the spiritual needs of the children. Church watchers, too, are easily scandalized by the noise children make coming into church, and the ' awful irreverence ' of the child who likes the doll or even the teddy bear to kneel down as well. Surely it was a touch of true religion when a child (now at rest) knelt before the image of our Lady and let off the only firework she possessed—a harmless ' sparkler.' It was easy to light it at the candles, and :

' Father, it was all stars.'   So too the boy who
has since become a priest was answering the
first stirrings of his vocation when one day he
took it in turn with his sister to sit in the
confessionals at Westminster Cathedral.   A
church that is always homely and welcoming,
and where there is an ordered freedom, and
not constant repression, is capable of being the
nursery of vocations.   Our Lord was, as some
think, recalling His childhood's days when He
drew one of His similes from the religious games
of children, ' Ye are like children playing in
the market place,' at weddings and funerals.

The church is naturally the place where the
children learn by what they see.   It should
be well equipped for them with the furniture
of religion.   Besides the sight of the holy sanctuary and the reverently cared for font and the
confessionals, they need a figure of the Baby
Jesus in His Holy Mother's arms, with a low
ledge where they can put their offerings of
flowers, or light a candle to show their love ;
and a crib at Christmas with the ox and the ass
and the shepherds complete, and the Stations
of the Cross, and a big crucifix and especially
His Presence in the Holy Sacrament.

Children enter eagerly into the Palm Procession and the Maundy Thursday Mass, and
the watch at the Altar of Repose.   ' Dear
child, when did you make your last confession ? '—' Please, Father, when Jesus was in
Gethsemane.'

The child learns by seeing and acting for himself ; and the priest will find much of the training done by the children, if the church is a place full of the material of teaching, and one in which religion is associated with joy and brightness and colour and music and beauty. The habit of coming into church in early childhood will stand them in good stead in the days when they find the difficulty of getting privacy for their prayers. By coming often into church they see the Sacraments and come to want them for themselves. ' Can I too go to Confession and have my sins forgiven ? ' ' Mother, I feel like Cinderella when you all go up to the altar and I have to stay behind.' Then if the priest can be there in church one day in the week after school, as the children come in he will find abundant opportunity for personal work, for hearing their confessions, for teaching them about prayer and the reading of the Bible.

THE MASS

It goes without saying that the children should come to Mass with their parents, and when this is the case the priest has not a great deal to be anxious about. But the majority of our children have to arrange about their religion for themselves, and so the priest must help them by making it not too difficult for them at Mass.

At the Parish Mass on Sundays the children

must not be at the back of the church, but should have some part reserved for them in front. Some of the hymns at least should be sufficiently well known for them to join in, and there should be a simple book for the younger ones, like *An Altar Book for Children* (Mowbrays), in which they can follow the Mass without difficulty.

If the children are together, very little disturbance is caused if they sit at the Prayer for the Church, or if they stand for part of the time, e.g. at the *Sursum Corda*, to avoid the fatigue of so much kneeling. In this case some one in charge will be useful, providing he does not fuss the children, overdo the directions given, or make the children feel uncomfortable by finding their places.

The Catechism and Sunday School

So far we have said a good deal about the kind of atmosphere which the priest aims at providing for the children of his parish. Now we must consider the actual work of instruction in the Faith.

The chief catechist ought always to be the priest, for he is ordered to ' instruct and examine so many children of his parish . . . as he shall think convenient openly in the church.' [1]

The number he is able to instruct will depend upon the size of his parish, and whether it is country or town. But, generally speaking,

[1] Preface, Prayer Book Catechism.

when he is able to, he should have the instruction of the boys and girls from about eleven to eighteen in his own hands. For the priest, what is known as the *Method of the Catechism* is the best method to adopt, especially if he does not adhere too rigidly to it.

The afternoon ' Catechism ' proceeds somewhat as follows :

The Assembly. The boys and girls enter freely, coming from their own homes, and take the places which are allotted to them annually. When the appointed time is come all stand and the Invocation is said. Card registers corresponding to each row are then marked by the monitors who sit at the end of the rows, and Catechism begins.

Notices and Admonitions. The catechist has then an opportunity for speaking about the time of Mass and Holy Communion, and anything else in which the members of the Catechism should be interested or take their part.

The Questioning. This exercise consists in the constant repetition in question and answer of what a Christian ought to know and believe. In a large building like a church it is better as a rule to have this repetition done by a few children who have volunteered to make the answers, and are forewarned of their turn to do so, rather than to risk nervous dread on the part of many.[1]

The Office. By placing the Office at this

[1] *The Church Catechism Simplified* (Mowbrays) is useful.

point a real change and relief is obtained before the attention has to be given to the Instruction. The Office may include, e.g., a short Act of Confession and Absolution ; Acts of Faith, Hope, and Love and Sorrow for Sin, and other prayers which every child ought to know ; a hymn, *Magnificat*, and Creed. The children are encouraged to take their share in the expenses and almsgiving by a regular collection.

The Instruction. An ordered course of teaching on the Creed, Morals, Prayer, Sacraments, Worship, the story of our Lord's life, and the story of the Church. Older children appreciate the authoritative teaching of the priest, but it is possible that groups might be formed for the Instruction under competent leaders. But the danger of spoiling the atmosphere involved in such a movement is obvious.

The Gospel Homily. The Gospel is usually read, while all present stand, and then a short appeal to the heart and conscience is made. But when the catechist is single-handed and gives the Instruction, it is better both for him and for the children if his appeal can be made as part of the Instruction, and the place of the Gospel and Homily be taken by devotions of a simple and informal kind, with a hymn sung kneeling.

The Dismissal then takes place in an orderly manner.

However much these exercises of the Questioning, the Instruction, and the Gospel Homily are used as a framework for the teaching which the priest gives to the children, the secondary exercises, the orderly assembly, the prayers, the hymns, the devotions, are the life and soul of it all.

The Society of the Method of the Catechism did an important work when it published Dupanloup's *Ministry of Catechizing* (National Society), and it should be read constantly as a treasure house of inspiration and illumination on the meaning of our work and the method to be used. The wonderful chapters on the secondary exercises, and on the necessity of a Catechism which sparkles and has a taste about it, need to be read again and again.

' Such,' Dupanloup says, ' is the course and order of a Catechism, but that is not enough. In order that the real end may be fully attained and the work on souls may be more certain there needs something more, something to relieve, and if I may venture to say so, to season all this, something which will give to all these excellent exercises of the Catechism a sort of taste, an aroma which shall make them loved and enjoyed. There needs, as it were, a breath of life circulating in all these different parts, an indefinable secret fire penetrating and animating them.

' To present the Catechism as an austere thing, always to have only a dry and hard manner, to make the Catechism a *triste*, wearisome thing without any attraction or life, this is not only a great mistake and a great want of skill, it is also to put in immense peril the future of these children, for these first impressions of religion can never be effaced.' [1]

Again, he speaks of the importance of the chapel, a place which the children will be eager

[1] Bk. II, Disc. viii.

to take care of, to adorn, and to decorate for festivals. ' Here,' he says, ' is a great secret, drawn out of the depths of a human heart. A place which any one has taken care of, which he has ornamented, which he has decorated himself, is a place he loves, because he has put something of his own there, and because in a certain way he sees himself there.'

So the members of the Catechism may be divided into wards or guilds, and encouraged to co-operate at festivals in decorating their portion of the church with their own pictures and flowers and lights. The wards may have their own banners for processions on special occasions, trimmed with garlands of flowers.

The atmosphere of the Catechism should be one of joy, peace, happiness, and devotion; and the secret of it all is a peace and happiness in the catechist himself. Fault-finding, irritability, and repressive measures are themselves the causes of disturbance.

But for reasons of age and numbers the priest cannot instruct all the children himself, so he must arrange as carefully as may be for those he cannot deal with.

Such a method as that described above might, if necessary, take place in a church hall or a schoolroom, with a little thought and arrangement. Here the catechist would be an assistant priest, or a sister, or a trained lay teacher.

The religious atmosphere can be fostered

by a simple arrangement of a shelf with a large coloured picture as reredos, a crucifix, lights, flowers, and some curtains. If chairs are not available, even desks can be put church wise. There is no reason why the children should not break up into groups for the Instruction, which can be graded and taught by a number of assistant teachers after the plan of any well-organized modern Sunday school. Many a Sunday school would work better on some such lines as these, just because of the greater atmosphere of prayer and devotion.

CONFIRMATION AND FIRST COMMUNION

If the priest has an ordered method in the training of his children, the preparation of children for Confirmation is simplified. The meetings of the Catechism provide in themselves the preparation for Confirmation, and the Guild of Perseverance afterwards. The few weeks which precede the Sacrament of Confirmation and the First Communion can be used for a preparation of a devotional character, with individual attention to each child's religious practices of Prayer, Confession, and Communion.

A great deal of the nervousness about Communion can be avoided by a reverent rehearsing of the act of receiving ; and the First Communion may be prepared for by a short Retreat on the Saturday afternoon, or two or three devotional services in the week before the

Communion. Those who have just been confirmed may receive their First Communion together, hymns being sung, veils worn, and everything being made as beautiful as possible. In the afternoon at Catechism there may be a Memorial of First Communion made with special hymns and devotions.

It is very possible that many of our children would be helped to persevere in their communions if they could be communicated in the week from the Reserved Sacrament without having of necessity to attend Mass.

Social Life and Fellowship

Where the boys and girls of a parish are learning their religion and worshipping together they will also need to fulfil the family life by meeting one another in the week. And the priest's aim will be to foster the family life. He will be seeking to form groups for social intercourse whenever he can. Amongst the members of the Catechism he may form a council to discuss with them any plans he may have from time to time. He may find a group of boys and girls who would form an orchestra and play the hymns at Catechism. His elder children will appreciate meeting one another in a simple weekly social for dancing and singing. For the younger ones provision can be made by Scouts and Guides, King's Messengers, Coral League, a Handicraft Guild, and folk dancing ; and whichever of these seem most possible, the delight of them will not be lessened by the fact that they are the expression of the family life of those who are already themselves loyal members of the family. So then, when all is said and done, the priest's work for his children is just this—to present before them as perfectly as he may the family life of the Holy Catholic Church, the kingdom of God our Father, and of His dear Son Jesus Christ.

PREACHING
By Francis Underhill

IV

PREACHING

IT is difficult to account for the perversity which almost until to-day has led to contempt for preaching of some Anglo-Catholics —clergy and laity. Even now, though things are gradually improving, this folly is not quite dead. You still hear men speaking of the sermon as though it were quite an inferior department of the life and work of the Church.[1]

No excuse can be found for this neglect of preaching either in the New Testament or in the history of the Catholic Church. Any one who reads the Gospels can see what our Lord thought of it. We are told that the earliest disciples went everywhere preaching the Word. The history contained in the Acts of the Apostles is an almost continuous narration of preaching expeditions, containing many outlines of sermons delivered. S. Paul gives

[1] I would venture, respectfully, to doubt the wisdom of those who divorce the sermon from the chief Sunday Mass. The result of this separation is commonly that the very persons who most need instruction seize the opportunity of escape from it. They go out after the service, while hardly any of those who have heard Mass earlier come for the sermon.

77

preaching a prominence the more remarkable in view of the emphasis always laid by the Church on the Sacraments, ' Be instant, in season, out of season, reprove, rebuke, exhort.'

It has been the same in all periods of the Church's history. The writings of the Christian Fathers were in very many cases first prepared in the form of sermons. Every great religious movement has used preaching for the propagation of the Faith. We need only remind ourselves of the beginnings of the work of the Franciscans, the Dominicans, the Jesuits, the Oratorians ; of S. Francis Xavier, of Pattison, of Wycliffe, Luther, John Wesley, and Pusey. Every revival of religion, every new impulse of missionary work, have depended upon preaching as careful as it was eloquent. Indeed, preaching precedes all other Church work. The first outpouring of the Holy Spirit was immediately followed by a series of enthusiastic sermons.

The whole sacramental life is prepared for by instruction. Yet, with incredible lack of prevision, exponents of the Catholic revival in England have depreciated the sermon in order to exalt the Mass, and have even discouraged attendance at Evensong with the same pathetic intention. We are now reaping the wretched fruit of this lamentable policy. Let us at least frankly repent of the absurdity which has so hurt that for which we stand, and recognize the essential importance of the sermon to-day.

THE PLACE OF PREACHING IN THE LIFE OF THE CHURCH TO-DAY

We justly complain in these days that there is in all classes a distressing ignorance of the true content of Catholicism—indeed of fundamental Christianity itself. We deplore the slight interest in religion in the daily and Sunday press. We complain that such articles as are published are often shallow and misinformed. We regret more keenly still that so many even of our best people are unable to give a reasoned reply to the many criticisms of the Faith with which they are faced at their work, in the street, in the railway train, among their friends.

What is the reason of all this ? It is very largely want of instruction. Most newspaper men do not know what Christianity is ; they have picked up somehow a garbled and attenuated form of it which they only understand sufficiently to be able to dogmatize on the subject.

Comparatively few people can be got to read books. They depend, therefore, more and more on the versions of religious truth presented to them by the journalists. But it goes even further than that. Most men and women will always need the human voice if they are to acquire any sufficient knowledge of Christian doctrine. Moreover, the desire to know grows with knowledge. If you can get a man

really interested in any branch of learning
he will come to hear more about it. He may
then be induced to read sound and simple
books bearing on subjects of which he has
heard something already. But he must be
started. We all find dullness in that of which
we know little. That is the fundamental
reason for the absurd fallacy that Christianity
is dull, unadventurous, and hostile to human
happiness.

Persuasive preaching will go far to provide
a remedy for all this. It would seem, too, that
nothing but ' good preaching ' will at present
draw people in the first place to church. But
enough of this. There should surely be no
need to enter a plea for the reconsideration of
the position of the sermon in the life of our
Church and Nation. I doubt if England needs
anything quite so much as a revived method of
preaching. It is the press, as we all know,
which influences most men and women to-day,
and the press itself would soon be reached and
influenced by more powerful preaching of
Christianity. Indeed it is a marked sign of
our times that any one who has prophetic gifts
generally gets ' a good press.' This is very
far from being contemptible. What we urgently need is a wide diffusion of Catholic
Christian teaching. Let us then get to grips,
first with the preparation for the sermon,
remote and immediate, and then with the
manner of its delivery.

Preparation for the Sermon

(*a*) *Remote Preparation*.

We will concentrate our attention in this section on the personality of the preacher, and the manner in which he prepares his general life for the delivery of his message.

Whether we like it or not, personality counts: or to put it better, it is character which tells everywhere and all the time. No doubt the unworthiness of the minister hinders not the effect of the Sacrament ; but the worthiness or unworthiness of the preacher must very deeply affect the reception of his preaching. This is just as true, in the long run, in the case of certain characteristics which the congregation would be quite incapable of appreciating, as in that of obvious outward goodness or wickedness.

The character of a preacher, therefore, may be deliberately developed with a view to his vocation ; and it is developed primarily by prayer and by the sacramental life of the Church in which he partakes. This must be far more than occasional or formal or professional prayer. It must mean an attitude of mind and spirit which inevitably forms his character, and enables him to draw others along the road he himself pursues. It is an attitude towards eternity, a way of living in the atmosphere of the infinite and the abiding ; a habit of acting, speaking, and thinking as in the great world

G

of God. In a word, it is what S. Paul means
when he speaks of 'our conversation'—that is,
'citizenship'—which is in heaven.

In these high matters we of the clergy differ
temperamentally as widely as other people do.
Some are called to move quite naturally on
heights which are inexpressible in human
words, but which, nevertheless, qualify a man
or woman to be a guide to others, by teaching
of the high places he has himself attained.
Most of us are less greatly blessed in this way.
Yet it is not easy to see how any one can
long continue to be a preacher of power who
does not habitually meditate on the mysteries
of God. Habitually; that is, not simply as
and when one is palpably moved to this kind
of spiritual exercise, but as a regular duty and
discipline of the whole life. We can only
preach convincingly of things which we have
heard and seen.

This kind of prayer life is largely built on
the habit of serious study. Men and women
will only accept permanently as a trusted
teacher a person of obvious holiness. But they
will also demand, though they may not know
it, the freshness which comes from sustained
learning. We of the clergy are far too ready
to exclaim that we can find no time for reading.
'We are so taken up,' we say, 'with urgent
pastoral work.' No doubt we are; but that
pastoral work is of no greater moment than the
preaching of the Gospel; and how can we go

on preaching intelligently unless our mind is constantly made wealthy by fresh ideas ?

Time *must* be found for reading. It is found by many men who are as busy as any can be. No doubt it means discipline of time, order and rule, a deliberate cutting down of the time given to the newspaper and novel. Yet those who have so planned their life have been astonished to find how many first-rate books the most hard-worked parish priest can get time to read in a comparatively short period of years. The result inevitably shows itself in more profound, more interesting, more inspiring sermons.

It may be possible to maintain on little reading or on a study merely of newspapers, novels, and the plays of the day, a certain type of popular preaching, but this will not do in the long run. A man who lives on this intellectual level will have to move quickly from church to church if he is to keep up his congregations. No ; sound and serious study lies at the foundation of all good preaching, for matter is what counts in the end. It is possible to succeed for a time by an elegant and agile flitting over the surface : an attractive manner and an easy flow of words may delight for a year or two ; but solidity wins. That strange body of hunters of popular sermons which exists in every place round about the more serious life of the Church may be held temporarily ; but the seekers after sound instruc-

tion will go where they can find what they
need.

(b) *Immediate Preparation*.

Not long ago I heard a young priest tell his
incumbent at nine o'clock on Saturday night
that he must now rush home and prepare his
sermon for the next morning! Levity of this
kind, though perhaps not often so shocking as
in this case, is far too common. Now putting
aside altogether the Godward aspect of preaching and its place in the Church, this kind of
thing is an insult to a congregation of Christian
people. In every church there are to be found
persons who, if not more learned, are at any
rate older and more experienced and holier than
the preacher. He is, to put it coarsely, paid to
give them of his best. Yet too often this kind
of preparation is what they get. No wonder
our congregations get irritated, bored, and
shocked.

The complacent young, or old, preacher
little realizes what that intelligent man under
the pulpit thinks of his obviously slipshod and
unprepared discourse. The parson thinks the
layman is taken in, and that because he himself
enjoys what he is saying the layman does also.
This is a great mistake. We are sufficiently
accustomed to the contemptuous manner in
which the layman almost universally speaks of
sermons. Is it not possible that he is sometimes right? We console ourselves by saying

that the layman is unreasonable. Is it less unreasonable in a priest to dot down two or three ' points ' on a sheet or two of notepaper, and to think that with such a preparation he can preach a sermon worth listening to ?

No ; if preaching needs a careful remote preparation of the personality of the preacher, it also needs a careful and lengthy immediate preparation. This is not only the case with sermons. Many of the men whose influence as public speakers lasts will take the trouble to write or type every word they mean to deliver. It may, or may not be, spoken exactly as it is written ; sometimes it may be phrased differently. Men who prepare carefully may even venture on an impromptu point from time to time without growing tedious. This is a matter of detail. The mistake lies in supposing that ' extempore ' speaking or preaching needs less preparation than what is written. It needs more preparation.

The effective speaker will think out his subject (having first chosen one) and will divide it up and arrange it ; he will see that his points follow one another in an intelligible order; he will take care that his corners are properly turned—that is, that his points dovetail into one another and do not produce the impression (except where it is intended) of violent change of subject. He will try to arrest his hearers by an interesting opening. He will plan for renewals of interest here and there which will draw back attention which may be beginning to flag. He will have a perceptible ending, which does not merely drag off into an unimpressive exit from the pulpit. He will dread, above all, the easy flux of words which is so terrible a snare to the self-satisfied. He will take care that whatever sin or abuse or mistake he may think right to attack, he is not simply negative. No sermon should be denunciatory throughout—men and women soon cease to respond to an unbroken flow of invective. The sermon should end, at any rate, on a note of hope. For instance, no sermon, even if it be one of a course, should deal exclusively with sin and its wages without a ray of hope. Somewhere there should be at least a hint that God would have all men to be saved.

But this is a digression. We have little room for detail in so short an essay. It is clear at any rate that the immediate preparation for a sermon involves a good deal of trouble, which assuredly ought to be given. It means deliberately fixing a time each week, or whenever needful, for the writing of the sermon. It means, further, the use of a man's unhurried intelligence. A sermon produced against time by a busy clergyman with a bursting brain and no time for anything in particular is not likely to help very much. I think it is difficult to exaggerate the amount of trouble which should be given to this outstanding exercise of our ministry.

THE DELIVERY OF THE SERMON

(a) *Sympathy with the Congregation.*

Many years ago, when I was a nervous young clergyman, an older friend tried to advise and console me as to my preaching. I remember that among other rules laid down he told me to think of the congregation as though they were so many rows of cabbages. He led me to hope that this plan would ensure calm of mind.

It was bad advice. If it could be followed it would soon ruin any person's power of public speaking ; for the root fact is that the speaker has before him not rows of cabbages, but rows of intelligent human beings ; and his duty, after invoking the Holy Spirit, is to look straight at them and see them as clearly as he can. He wants to get into the closest possible sympathy with them. He must enter as far as he can into their minds, and understand as perfectly as he can how they are taking what he is saying. He must therefore, probably almost unconsciously, watch their faces and note their movements. He should be quick to feel loss of hold, and to realize the signs of growing inattention when they come. For if he by speaking gives something to the congregation, so they give or withhold from him all kinds of help and encouragement. This is none the less real because perhaps no single person in the congregation is consciously aware of it.

The duty of the speaker is to hold the greatest

possible number of his hearers and to keep them
listening. This necessitates much sensitiveness, which again is only partly conscious, and
is not in the least inconsistent with the abiding
sense of the Holy Spirit and of dependence
on Him.

Congregations differ widely. Some are alert,
friendly, and perceptive. To use a vulgar
proverb, they ' give as good as they get.' Some
are very different ; they are stodgy, supine,
unresponsive ; the most practised speaker will
find it hard to talk to them. There is no
give and take ; or rather it is all give and no
take. I do not know any more exacting task
than preaching the Three Hours' Service on
Good Friday to a congregation of this type.

A visiting preacher of discernment quickly
feels the atmosphere of a congregation. He
can tell from it fairly accurately what the relation
is between the parish clergy and the congregation, and what kind of preaching they generally
get. He will know if they are persistently
scolded ; if a narrow type of theology has
made them suspicious of other ideas and other
methods ; he may miss any sign of a spirit of
devotion, and find the atmosphere frigid or
hostile. On the other hand, he is very quickly
at home where there is Christian love and trust
between clergy and people of the parish. If
they are accustomed to listen gladly to their
regular preachers, they will give a generous
welcome to a visitor.

(*b*) *The Manner of the Preacher.*

Much depends also upon the manner of the
preacher and his way of speaking to the laity.
I have known congregations of good people
irritated beyond endurance by perpetual scolding. It is said that nothing succeeds like
success. It is perfectly true, on the other hand,
that loud and prolonged proclamation of disappointment from the pulpit lamentably fails
to succeed in the object presumably desired.
Pulpit scolding quickly becomes a habit, and
like most other bad habits is unrecognized by
the offender. It is only too quickly realized
by everybody else. The inevitable results are
a diminishing congregation and a broken-
hearted priest.

I do not think it is unfair to say that this is
a danger which particularly besets some of the
younger clergy. The name of the preacher
in the ordinary parish church is not generally
advertised, and therefore the normal congregation is present at most services. The good
people in any church will often put up with a
good deal from their assistant clergy which they
do not like, because after all the incumbent is
at the back of things. This often misleads
the younger priests. I write with shame, as
myself an offender. I remember when, as an
assistant priest, I was advertised to preach a
Lent course on Sunday mornings in the church
I was serving, and was horrified to find that,
though usually well filled, it was half empty on

the first Sunday. The truth was that I had
been for some time irritating the congregation
by ill-mannered scolding.

The salutary and unpleasant lesson hurt
badly at the time, but I hope I may have learnt
some wisdom from it. It is wretched to sit
in a congregation and feel all round one a sense
of anger and outrage, produced by ineffective
heckling, or by a bland air of superiority in the
preacher which is hardly less exasperating. I
do not think I exaggerate. The office of the
preacher is one of signal difficulty, and it must
always be remembered that he cannot be
answered. This is perhaps one of the most
salient facts about the use of the pulpit. Many
a sermon would be exceedingly useful as the
opening speech of a debate. As an isolated
utterance it irritates. It cannot be, I suppose ;
but how much good it would do us and how
greatly it would improve our preaching if we
could sometimes hear a reply to it.

Further, it is important that we who have to
preach should know what beseems us and what
does not. One man can employ methods
which are ridiculous in another. He may
express himself naturally in ways which
would be offensive in his nearest friend. The
style of a great preacher, while it perfectly
befits him, is probably absurd in his imitators.
We are never more truly effective than when
we are our natural selves : when we say what
we have to say with reliance upon the Spirit

of God, with simplicity, and as far as possible
without self-consciousness. It is difficult not
to catch mannerisms from other preachers ;
from our own colleagues, for instance, whom we
often hear preaching. It is wise to be watchful,
and not to wear borrowed plumes, however
becoming they may be to another.

May I dare to say that a special danger
besets eloquent missioners ? Too frequent
preaching of this special kind is apt to lead to
a growing exaggeration of manner. What was
once telling and appropriate becomes tame to
the preacher himself. He feels he must be
more stirring, or his message will not go home.
And so he shouts and bangs the pulpit and
over-states his case, and is in danger, not
of moving his congregation, but of leaving
them much embarrassed. It is surely wise
that preachers who have the great responsibility
of this kind of evangelization should be given
long periods of quiet retirement for recollection
and prayer.

(c) *Nervousness.*

' What can I do to get rid of my terrible
nervousness ? ' so many a young preacher asks
his elders. My answer is : ' Do you want to
get rid of it ? ' No doubt there is a kind of
nervousness which paralyses, but this is far less
common than the nervousness which humiliates
and braces if it is recognized as a blessing and
used for its right purpose.

I think if we were to ask many of our greatest speakers how long it took them to get over their nervousness they would answer : ' I never have got over it.' They would say that they are horribly nervous before every speech they make and every sermon they preach. They dread the moment when the chairman calls upon them to stand up and address the meeting. They tremble every time they mount the pulpit. But it is probably just that apparent weakness which is their real strength ; which makes their power permanent. It does much to prevent personal dogmatism and that cock-sureness of manner which alienates sympathy and attention ; at any rate the attention of men.

It is nervousness which makes a man take trouble, and always more trouble, over his preparation, because he knows he cannot be sure of himself at the critical moment unless he has done all he can to be ready for it. It is salutary nervousness which is the final preventive of that self-satisfaction which bars the way to further progress. But the finest use nervousness has is spiritual discipline : it throws the preacher back again and again into reliance upon the Holy Spirit of God whose grace alone is sufficient for us and whose strength is made perfect in weakness.

I think if we dared to ask the greatest preachers about the final preparation of all for their sermon we should find that the last thought before they stand up and begin to speak is an almost agonized appeal for pardon for unworthiness and sin, and a prayer to be filled with divine power. While at those dark moments, which come sometimes to all of us in the middle of a sermon, when memory fails and utter depression falls on us, and we feel the attention of the congregation growing less and less ; again at that very moment we are driven to supplicate without words for that inspiration of the Holy Ghost which is the only true refuge in our nervousness and distress.

CONCLUSION

Hitherto we have dealt with two aspects of the sermon : the preparation for it—remote and immediate—and the manner of its delivery. A vast number of interesting and important matters have had perforce to be omitted. It will be well, however, to conclude with a few thoughts on one side of the preacher's preparation which is also exceedingly important.

The preacher who will most permanently help those to whom he speaks is the best pastor. His is the influence which counts, and he is the preacher who finds the cost the greatest. It is no disparagement of the preacher of occasional missions or the conductor of retreats to say that his is a comparatively easy task. His message is fresh and therefore attractive ; his personality and his voice are new ; he comes to do his great piece of work, and then he disappears again. Resolutions are made, men and women are delivered from sin and are roused to fresh efforts. The preacher only returns now and then on a visit—his is not the duty of carrying on.

The parish priest has been among his people for years, and has thankfully made way for the distinguished stranger who visits the parish for ten days or a fortnight. But when the mission is over he must take up again his task of teaching. If he has the trust of his people they will hear him gladly and welcome his familiar voice once more. Then the effects of the mission will not soon fade away, for it is the years as they pass which form the real test of a man's preaching.

There are many faithful priests whose people always love to hear them, because they are sure, though they may grow ever so familiar, that the mind and heart of their pastor remain fresh. He stands at his altar representing his people before God ; he hears their confessions ; he prays, meditates, studies. His interior life, only partly guessed at even by those who know him best, keeps him above that weariness and disappointment which must always be a temptation to the most faithful parish priest. He will not shrink from reproof when it is necessary, but his love for his people will keep him from scolding them. A wise preacher will never make personal references in his preaching unless it be to praise the departed ; but his constant visiting, his sympathetic touch with the conditions in which his people live, his knowledge of the children whom he has brought up in the faith, added to the sound learning he gets from his books, will always keep his preaching fresh and interesting. Such wise and disciplined instruction is the outcome of years of growing intimacy.

This is no mere ideal. In town and country, preachers are to be found whose sermons do not pall even after many years. Personal holiness and sincerity, sound and consistent reading, respect and love for his hearers, knowledge of human nature and experience of the world, courage, intellectual and moral honesty; these, based upon an intimate knowledge of the Gospel of our Lord Jesus Christ, and on self-forgetfulness in the message to be delivered and enthusiasm for the Catholic Faith, will enable us to teach and help those to whom we are sent. The fire which burns in the preacher's heart will kindle in the lives of his people.

(NOTE.—I have not dealt specifically with the Broadcast Sermon, because it is still in the experimental stage. In spite of obvious disadvantages it exercises a growing influence, on the whole for good.)

PASTORAL VISITATION OF THE SICK AND WHOLE

By CHARLES NEWELL LONG

H

V

PASTORAL VISITATION OF THE
SICK AND WHOLE

IN all his pastoral dealings with his flock the priest will derive his main inspiration from the example and teaching of the Good Shepherd, from whom he received his own commission as a shepherd of souls. He will also study the examples and teaching of other great pastors such as the Apostles of our Lord and those who in every successive age have exercised a faithful ministry.

First, and chiefest, we have the example of our Blessed Lord, Who never lost an opportunity of dealing with individual souls. ' I am the Good Shepherd and know My sheep.' ' He calleth His own sheep by name.' We think of Him calling men, one by one, to be His disciples. We think of Him training them, one by one, with such patience and love, to be His Apostles ; commending them, rebuking them, correcting their mistakes, and bearing with all their want of faith and misunderstanding of His teaching. Or we think of Him dealing with individual sinners such as the woman of Samaria and the woman taken in

adultery, and with individual penitents such
as the woman in the house of Simon the
Pharisee and Zacchaeus the rich publican. We
remind ourselves how He, Who has taught us
the parables of the Lost Sheep and the Lost
Coin and the Prodigal Son, never gave any one
up so long as there was any possibility of saving
him from his wilfulness and sin ; how even
the traitor Judas was tenderly dealt with until
the end. We recall how He never shrank
from inflicting pain upon those whom He loved
when He knew it to be for their good. The
' Get thee behind Me Satan,' addressed to
S. Peter ; the ' Ye know not what manner of
spirit ye are cf,' addressed to S. James and
S. John ; and the firm though tender restoration of S. Peter to his apostolate by the Sea of
Tiberias are sufficient indications of this.

Now and again we are told of special indications of His love for individuals : ' Jesus, be-
holding him, loved him ' ; ' now Jesus loved
Mary and Martha and Lazarus ' ; and ' the
disciple whom Jesus loved '—but we must
not infer from this that the Master made
favourites. It was only that the intense love
which He felt for each and all betrayed itself
at times by its intensity. And how eager He
was to buy up the opportunity as it presented
itself ! Nicodemus came to Him by night ;
the blind beggar, whose sight He had restored,
He sought out and found after the Jews had
cast him out of the synagogue ; weariness did

not prevent Him from using His opportunity with the woman of Samaria ; agonizing suffering did not make Him forget His Mother and S. John as He hung upon the Cross. And the children were His special care.

It was with such an example before him that S. Paul at Ephesus ' by the space of three years ceased not to admonish every one night and day with tears.' It was because of this that he could testify unto the elders of the Church that he was ' pure from the blood of all men.' ' For,' as he said, ' I shrunk not from declaring unto you the whole counsel of God.'

We have here an illuminating picture of the pastoral ministrations of the great Apostle. In a similar manner in his first letter to the Thessalonians he calls them to witness, ' and God also, how holily and righteously and unblameably we behaved ourselves towards you that believe : as ye know how we dealt with each one of you, as a father with his own children, exhorting you, and encouraging you, and testifying, to the end that ye should walk worthily of God, Who calleth you into His own kingdom and glory.' And, once more, in writing to the Colossians he speaks of ' admonishing *every* man and teaching *every* man in all wisdom, that we may present *every* man perfect in Christ.' Here is the mark of the true pastor of souls who is never content with dealing with men in the mass but who feels compelled to deal with each one, one by one, as a father with

his own children, admonishing every man and teaching every man, that he may present every man perfect in Christ.

The Importance of Pastoral Work

Every priest is called to be an under-shepherd of the Good Shepherd. However skilled he may be in organizing a parish, however eloquent his preaching may be, however generous he may be in ministering to the bodily needs of his flock, however many social attractions he may provide for them, he will be failing in the main object of his ministry unless his heart is set on dealing with individuals, one by one. It was laid upon him as a solemn charge at the hour of his ordination to the priesthood :

Have always therefore printed in your remembrance, how great a treasure is committed to your charge. For they are the sheep of Christ, which he bought with his death, and for whom he shed his blood. The Church and Congregation whom you must serve, is his Spouse, and his Body. And if it shall happen the same Church, or any Member thereof, to take any hurt or hindrance by reason of your negligence, ye know the greatness of the fault, and also the horrible punishment that will ensue. Wherefore . . . see that you never cease your labour, your care and diligence, until you have done all that lieth in you, according to your bounden duty, to bring all such as are or shall be committed to your charge, unto that agreement in the faith and knowledge of God, and to that ripeness and perfectness of age in Christ, that there be no place left among you, either for error in religion, or for viciousness in life

THE VISITATION OF THE SICK AND DYING

It would be difficult to exaggerate the importance of pastoral ministrations to the sick and dying. The visitation of the sick affords a precious opportunity for dealing with individual souls at a time when they are often, although not always, peculiarly susceptible to spiritual influences. It is also of great value for the opportunity it affords of bringing influence to bear upon the relatives and friends of those who are sick. A priest who is faithful and sympathetic in his ministry to the sick and dying will win the gratitude and affection of their friends and will forge links which may never be broken.

Yet this branch of his ministry is often one of extraordinary difficulty. ' Nothing,' it has been said, ' tries the nerve and the faith of a young priest like the ministry to the sick.' He has need of patience and tact on the one hand and of firmness and courage on the other. If he should fail either in tact or in courage he may lose an opportunity which may never recur again. ' Rub lightly,' said Bishop King, ' but remember that if you rub too lightly the match will not light at all.'

In the sick room, if anywhere, the priest must be recognized as a true man of God, a man of prayer. Here may be emphasized the

importance of faithful pastoral dealings with
those who are in health, in order that they may
welcome the priest as one who is already their
friend whenever they are sick. The parish
priest should also frequently impress upon his
people the importance of letting him hear in
good time of any cases of serious illness in
order that he may visit them before they are
too ill to profit by his ministrations.

There is a prevalent superstition that the
clergyman should not be called in to visit the
sick until there is little or no hope of their
recovery, and in many places the reception of
Holy Communion by the sick is regarded as if
it were necessarily an immediate preparation
for death. Even the asking of the prayers
of the Church on behalf of those who are
sick is often confined to the cases of those
who are dangerously ill, and many who
would greatly value this bond of fellowship with other members of the congregation to which they belong are deprived of the
privilege.

The priest himself will make his ministrations to the sick a matter of special thought
and prayer. He will have his list of sick people
whom he is visiting, and will pray for them
constantly and regularly and will invite others
to do the same.

The sick and dying may be divided into two
main classes : (1) those who need conversion,
and (2) those who need edification.

The Unconverted

Amongst these there will be many of whom he has had little or no previous knowledge. When he is called upon to visit one of these he will, whenever it is possible, make a few preliminary inquiries as to the spiritual and temporal condition of the sick man before he enters the sick room. He will ascertain, for instance, whether he has been baptized and confirmed ; whether he is a regular communicant or has lapsed from Communion ; what kind of life he has led (although such an inquiry should be made with caution) ; what his physical and mental condition is ; and also, and this is of special importance, whether he is supposed to be in immediate danger of death. On entering the house, and especially in the sick room, he will let it be seen that, like the doctor, he has come with a definite purpose in view, and that he knows his ' business ' ; he will take charge of the case and expect to have his directions carried out.

With rare exceptions, as, for instance, when the sick man is too ill or too nervous for this to be done on the first occasion, the priest will ask to be left alone with him, and will do his best to win his confidence by establishing some point of contact. This can often be done on a first visit, but sometimes it requires several visits to be paid before confidence is gained. In the Life of Manning we are told that he

was greatly discouraged by his failure to
establish any point of contact with an unin-
structed shepherd whom he was visiting. One
day, however, he took with him a picture of
the Good Shepherd which he laid upon the
bed. The man seemed as unresponsive as
ever, but, at the end of the visit, when Manning
was picking up the picture, the man murmured,
' Don't take it away.' Some days after, when
the man died, the picture was found next to his
heart. The repetition of a well-known hymn
will often be helpful. In this work of winning
confidence, as indeed in all visitation of the
sick, an experienced lay-helper is often of great
assistance, although a caution may here be
necessary against making use of untrained or
indiscreet helpers in such work.

When confidence has once been gained,
every effort should be made to quicken or to
deepen penitence. The complete lack of any
sense of sin on the part of many of those to
whom they are called upon to minister is the
disheartening experience of all priests. How
often have we heard some such expression as,
' I have never done any one any harm ! '

The Uninstructed

It is obvious that in many cases the necessary
preliminary before any sense of sin can be
aroused is some definite instruction about God
and His claims. If time allows some such
careful instruction should precede any insist-

ence upon the need of penitence. The Order
for the Visitation of the Sick lays great stress
upon the need of penitence, but not before the
priest has been instructed to question the sick
man about the reality of his faith in God. It is
also helpful in this connection to emphasize the
importance of sins of omission. Such parables
as those of the Talents, the Ten Virgins, the
Last Judgement, and the Wedding Feast will
serve to bring this home to the conscience.

When the way has been prepared the priest
must not be afraid to strike home, even at the
risk of giving offence. There is often too
much softness and indefiniteness in our ministrations. People expect straight dealing from
us and do not respect us for our over consideration for their feelings. ' The hungry
sheep look up and are not fed.' We are apt
to forget that ' one of the divinest qualities of
the infinite love is its capacity for inflicting pain.
It would rather see the loved one dead than
dishonoured, tortured than stained.'

If a priest has a true love of souls in his heart
it will inevitably reveal itself to those to whom
he ministers. *Ama et fac quod vis* is a saying
of S. Augustine. There is value in a single
phrase solemnly repeated ; some such phrase
as ' You belong to God ' has often effected a
conversion. In the case of those who have
long neglected prayer it is of great value for
the priest to get them to repeat simple prayers
after him, for instance Acts of Faith, Hope,

Love, and Contrition. It is difficult to over-estimate the effect of the reopening of the lips of prayer after years of silence.

A story is told of Canon Body who, as a young man, once assisted at an after-meeting during a Moody and Sankey Mission. One of the missioners came to him afterwards and asked him why it was that, as he had observed, all the people whom he had been interviewing went away with a different expression on their faces from that on those who had been dealt with by the other helpers. Body replied that he did not know why it should be so, unless it was that he got the inquirers to pray *with* him while, as he had noticed, the other helpers prayed *for* them. It may be noted here that in praying for the sick (or those in health) it is desirable to pray without a book, using ex-tempore prayers or prayers learned by heart which may be adapted for the purpose. Well-known passages of Scripture should also be committed to memory.

A short written or type-written prayer may be left with the sick person to be used by him. By these and similar means the way may be prepared for a true conversion of the heart to God, to be followed by a humble and sincere confession of sins.

PREPARATION FOR CONFESSION

The priest should be prepared to assist the penitent in making his confession. With simple folk some such method as the following may be used. 'You know that you are seriously ill?' 'You believe in God our Father, in Jesus Christ His Son, Who became Man for us, and that He died to save you; and you believe in God the Holy Ghost, Who has come to help you to love and serve God?' 'You know that you are a sinner; do you wish to be made sure of your forgiveness?' 'Will you let me help you to remember your sins?' A brief inquiry should then follow as to common sins of the class to which the sick person belongs; sins against God, his neighbour, and himself; sins of omission; the possibility of self-deception.

In *Notes on the Absolution of the Sick and Dying* Linton points out the value of an illustration in this connection. ' I have sometimes,' he says, ' used the true story of a priest who, visiting a dying woman, found her at peace and confident of salvation. He presently reminded her of a quarrel she had with her sister; whereupon the dying woman, raising herself in bed, exclaimed, " Never mention that woman's name to me," showing thus a state of malice which must have destroyed her soul.' Having elicited a true confession the priest may ask, ' Shall I give you God's message of forgiveness?' and Absolution may then be conferred.

A priest friend of the writer who is working in a country parish discovered that an old man whom he was visiting on what proved to be his

death-bed had been confirmed in his youth
and had received Communion. On inquiring
whether he would like to receive Communion
again the reply came, ' Oh yes, I *should*.'
' Would you like me to help you to prepare
for Holy Communion ? ' ' Oh yes, I *should*.'
After a brief preparation the priest said to
him, ' As God's minister I am able to give
you His message of forgiveness : would you
like me to do so ? ' ' Oh yes, I *should*.' After
he had received the Absolution the old man
said, ' I've been wanting to get that off my
mind for a while.' The next day he received
his communion, and as the priest bade him
' Good-bye ' the old man raised his hand to his
lips and kissed it.

Most of what has been said so far has pre-
supposed that the patient is in no immediate
danger of death. The priest, however, is
often called upon to minister to those who
have only a few days or even hours to live.
In such cases he must pray earnestly for guidance and do the best that is possible under
the circumstances. When the conscience has
already been aroused and time is short the
confession of one mortal sin is sufficient matter
for the conferring of Absolution.

When the patient is conscious but speech-
less communication may be established by the
pressure of the hand or by sign ; when he is
unconscious or only half-conscious conditional
Absolution should be bestowed provided that

there is reason to suppose that he is penitent and would desire to receive it.

In justification of this practice, Gaume relates how the Archbishop of Besançon, wishing to avoid risk of the validity of the Sacrament, had forbidden his priests to give Absolution to the dying if no request, or sufficient sign of a desire to confess, had been made. The prelate himself, however, was suddenly attacked by sickness, and in the course of it wished earnestly to confess, but found himself powerless to make known his desire either by word or sign. He recovered his health, and revoked his former instructions, enjoining that the dying who had lived as Christians should be absolved even though they should make no request or sign of desiring to confess, since it is very probable that grace may produce in them the conditions necessary for Absolution.[1]

(NOTE.—For the whole subject of the Absolution of the sick and dying see R. C. Linton, quoted above, published by Longmans ; and Belton, *Manual for Confessors*, published by Knott.)

THE INSTRUCTED

In considering the case of those who are already instructed in the Faith they may also be divided into two main classes : (1) the partially, and (2) the fully instructed ; and those who come under either of these headings may also need conversion if, during health, they have fallen away from Church and the Sacraments. *Ceteris paribus* the same course of treatment may be adopted with these as has been already

[1] Linton, pp. 72–3.

outlined. Confidence must first be established, after which the conscience must be aroused and the soul prepared for the reception of sacramental grace. The more fully instructed the sick person may be the more easy will it be to go directly to the point, and to introduce the subject of Confession at once. Care should be taken to ascertain whether previous confessions have been well and duly made, and the penitent should be instructed to confess first such sins as are weighing most heavily on his conscience, after which the priest may assist him by questioning if he is able to bear it. The greatest difficulty may arise with the partially-instructed, who are often influenced by Protestant prejudices against Confession ; but wherever there is a true love for Christ, however ill-informed it may be, it should not be difficult to lead the soul to sincere penitence and a desire for Absolution. It should be borne in mind that prejudice is commonly associated with some particular idea or even phrase, and that when those are avoided the desired result may be attained.

The Faithful

The case of those who need edification rather than conversion may now be considered. This will, of course, include those already mentioned who have been brought to a true conversion as well as others who may not be thought to need conversion, although a priest will be wise not to assume that his ' best ' people do not need to unburthen their consciences. There are sad cases of those who have been going regularly to Confession for years but have always concealed some sin of their past lives, and so have made false confessions. Such as these may, under the discipline of sickness and the opportunity of more intimate relations with their parish priest, welcome the opportunity of making a true repentance.

The Exhortation in the Visitation Office points the sufferer to the Cross, and whenever the suffering seems to be inevitable ' there should be no greater comfort to Christian persons than to be made like unto Christ, by suffering patiently adversities, troubles, and sicknesses.'

The sick and suffering are always subject to the temptation to consider that they are useless and a burthen to others. It is a great comfort to them to be instructed how to offer their sufferings, in union with the Passion of our Lord, on behalf of others. This is the teaching of S. Paul when he says : ' Now I rejoice in my sufferings for your sake, and fill up on my part that which is lacking of the afflictions of Christ in my flesh *for His body's sake, which is the Church.*' A woman lying in hospital and suffering agonies of pain was overheard to exclaim from time to time, ' I offer this for . . .,' mentioning the needs of those in whom she was interested. She had learnt how to make her sufferings of use to others.

I

Apart from this, the heroic endurance of pain and suffering is of itself one of the most powerful arguments for the reality of the faith which inspires it, and has a strong influence with those who are brought into contact with the sufferer. A priest may do much to alleviate the suffering and loneliness of those whom he visits in sickness by telling them of other sufferers for whom they may intercede, and by supplying them with information about the needs of the Church and in particular of their own parish, and so linking them up with the wider fellowship of the Church. If they are taught to practise Invocation of the Saints they will gain by that a still wider outlook. We do not sufficiently realize the intense spiritual loneliness of many of those who are cut off from an active life. Much may be done to mitigate this in the ways which have already been indicated, and sometimes also by a discreet choice of visitors who are not mere gossips.

SPIRITUAL HEALING

But while recognizing that, under our present conditions in an imperfect world, much sickness may be inevitable, it would be a cruel injustice to withhold from the sick the hope of recovery. The Visitation Office fails conspicuously in this respect. The revival of Spiritual Healing needs to be carefully safeguarded against abuse, but every priest should encourage the sick to look for bodily healing not only by medical but also by spiritual means. The influence of mind over body is universally acknowledged in these days, and there must be few priests who cannot point to remarkable instances of recovery from illness as the result of prayer, laying on of hands, the anointing of the sick, and the reception of the Sacraments. While the administration of the Sacrament of Holy Unction (termed ' Extreme ' Unction because it is the last of the anointings of the Church and not because it is administered *in extremis*), according to Western usage, is confined to those who are in danger of death,[1] there is precedent for the use of oil for the purpose of healing apart from its more specifically sacramental use. It is probable that many individuals, whether priests or lay men or women, possess what is known as ' the gift of healing ' ; and, apart from such natural gifts, our Lord still heals the bodily ills of His people through the ministrations of His Church. But this is a subject which cannot be dealt with at length in the space at our disposal.

Administration of the Sacraments

Provision should be made for regular and frequent administration of the Sacraments of Penance and of Holy Communion to the sick

[1] The writer has had personal experience of several complete recoveries after the administration of the Sacrament of Holy Unction, in cases where, humanly speaking, recovery had seemed impossible.

if so desired. It is lamentable that sick persons who have been regular in making their confessions and communions while in health should be deprived of the opportunity of receiving the Sacraments when ill, or should only receive them at infrequent and irregular intervals. Priests do not always realize that if they are not asked to administer the Sacraments it is not because the sick do not desire them, but rather out of consideration for themselves. They should be at pains to make it clear that they consider it to be one of their primary duties and privileges to bring the Blessed Sacrament to the sick. Of all the means by which the spiritual loneliness of the sick can be alleviated this is the most valued, for it not only brings them into union with our Lord, but also links them up with the congregation of which they are members and with the Communion of Saints living and departed.

The sick should be instructed that in cases of severe illness where there is danger of death they are released from the obligation of keeping the fast before Communion. Other difficulties which arise from time to time about keeping the fast should be brought to the notice of the priest.

Whenever the Sacrament of Holy Communion is administered care should be taken to provide the outward appointments and so to make the administration as reverent as possible. Undue fussiness should, however, be avoided in making the necessary preparations, and due regard should be paid to the physical and nervous conditions of the patient. In cases of severe sickness the priest should shorten the administration. The practice of reserving the Blessed Sacrament makes Communion possible in many cases where a long service would be out of the question, and in cases of less serious illness where the patient is able to go to church but unable to bear the fatigue of being present throughout a Mass, Communion may be given at any hour from the Reserved Sacrament.

In administering the Sacraments in hospital wards a screen can always be placed round the sick bed when a confession is being heard or when Communion is being given. This may not always be desirable when several people are being communicated in the same ward, but it is usually desirable when only one or two are being communicated. In cases where there is danger of nausea a very small particle may be administered. For full directions in case of infectious diseases the reader is referred to Part II, chapter i, in Belton's *Manual for Confessors*.

NOTE.—Where facilities are readily given for communicating the sick with the Reserved Sacrament there may be considerable numbers of sick communions. One priest of a working-class parish in Birmingham told the writer that for a number of weeks in succession he had an average of thirteen or fourteen sick communions

each week ; other priests in similar parishes
have an average of from five or six to nine
or ten each week.

SOME SUGGESTIONS

A few suggestions may here be given which
may be helpful in dealing with cases of chronic
sickness. There are sick persons who are
sufficiently well to value and profit by a course
of definite instruction to be given them week
by week. Short of this a course of Scriptural
or devotional reading may be suggested to
them, or a short passage of Scripture or from
some devotional book may be read to them.
Care should be taken to see that they have
objects of devotion, such as a crucifix or sacred
picture, to look at.

It is a common experience in sickness to be
unable to concentrate the thoughts in prayer ;
the sick should be instructed to use short
prayers and aspirations, and the rosary will be
found to be especially helpful. With some of
the better instructed the priest may occasionally
use the Visitation Office throughout, asking
them to read it through themselves before he
does so.

The priest should be careful to ascertain
whether the sick are realizing their responsibilities with regard to their temporal posses-
sions. He should inquire whether debts have
been paid, and should exhort the more well-to-
do to be liberal to the poor. As a matter of

common justice he should insist on the obligation to make a will, for, even when the sick
person has little to dispose of, many heart-
burnings may be avoided after a death if care
has been exercised in the disposal.

The priest should be regular and punctual
in his visits to the sick. He should realize
that his visits are events of real importance in
what is too often a monotonous existence, and
that any failure to keep an appointment may
lead to anxious expectation or fretful uncertainty. When he finds it impossible to keep an
appointment he should send a message. He
should avoid paying his visits at inconvenient
hours, as, for instance, when the patient is
fatigued after the visits of the doctor or nurse,
or in the late evening when the excitement of
a visit may prevent the patient from sleeping.
He should always be on his guard against tiring
the patient unnecessarily. He should avoid
noise of any kind in the sick room, and should
not sit on or touch the bed. Argument should
be studiously avoided, and the priest should
be on his guard against false encouragement
on the one hand, and over-commiseration on
the other. He should realize what a potent
factor cheerfulness of demeanour is towards a
patient's recovery.

The question is often asked whether a man
ought to be told that he is dying. This is not
a question that can be answered without regard
to the condition of the patient. Those whose

faith is strong can usually be told of the
approach of death without danger, and have a
right to be told the truth, but there are others to
whom the knowledge, if imparted, would only
increase their suffering and possibly hasten
their end.   And it should be remembered that
doctors are not infallible and that many sick
persons have entirely recovered who had been
thought to be at death's door, and who, had they
been told that they were dying, would have
ceased to fight for life.   If a man is obviously
ignorant of his danger and careless about his
spiritual condition he should be told that he
is seriously ill, and urged to penitence and
prayer.

Whenever it is possible the priest should
have an understanding with the doctor, and
work with him.   Sometimes difficulties arise
between priests and medical men or nurses,
but these can usually be surmounted by a
personal interview if the priest is reasonable
and tactful.   All priests have not these virtues,
and there are cases where a doctor is justified
in keeping the priest away from the sick room.

When ministering to those who are at the
point of death frequent short visits should be
paid rather than longer ones.   Care should be
taken to administer the Sacrament of Holy
Unction and the *Viaticum* before the dying
person is too weak to receive them.   Short
Acts of Faith, Hope, Love, and Contrition ;
holy aspirations, such as the use of the holy

Name, with frequent pauses between them, should be used. Familiar prayers and hymns and psalms of penitence, and also of hope and confidence, may be used.

When the soul is passing, the commendatory prayer from the Visitation Office may be used, or the beautiful commendatory prayers and litanies from the old Sarum or Latin rites, translations of which may be found in many books of devotion. As has already been indicated, it is not always realized that the soul is often conscious when no outward indication of consciousness is visible, and the presence of the priest during the last hours of life may be of the greatest service and comfort.

VISITATION OF THE WHOLE [1]

Much that has been said already will apply with equal force to the visitation of those who are in health ; for the main purposes will be the same, namely, conversion and edification. The priest should never rest content until he has done all that lies in his power ' to restore to God's grace the image of God in every person in his parish.' [2]

The utility of parochial visitation should be

[1] The writer's experience has been almost entirely confined to large artisan parishes in great cities, and he cannot claim to speak of country parishes or for town parishes of a different type.

[2] Bishop Edward King.

apparent.   A priest will never know his people
thoroughly until he has visited them in their
own homes.   He visits them for his own sake
as much as for theirs.   His preaching will fail
in its effect without the mutual knowledge
gained by visiting.   He has opportunities
afforded him of personal dealing with souls
which otherwise would never be open to him.
Nor is this only so in the case of those who have
never come to church.   As he visits the faithful
members of his flock in their own homes he
gains an insight into their lives and characters
which not even the confessional can give to
him.   For he sees them in their everyday
surroundings and is thus enabled to estimate
the kind of trials and temptations which they
have to face.

But he needs to be systematic in his visitation.   Indiscriminate visiting involves a great
waste of time and energy.   It is necessary that
he shall have a definite plan, beginning with
the homes of those who are in some way
attached to the Church, but not confining himself to them.   A certain amount of house-to-
house visitation is good, and should be undertaken by priests who are not too fully occupied
with special visits of one kind or another.
The longer a priest remains in one parish the
more of this special visiting will fall to his lot,
and the less time he will have to give to more
general visiting.

Circumstances alter cases, but, if the importance of parochial visitation is realized, a considerable time should be devoted to it. As a rough guide it may be suggested that two or three hours on four or five afternoons or evenings a week is not too much. The priest should school himself to the discipline of starting out punctually from his study at a definite time. Before doing so he will have formed his plan of visits to be paid that afternoon or evening, and will have refreshed his memory about the circumstances of the families which he is about to visit. For this purpose he will keep a record and possibly a card-index. He will carry a small note-book in which he may unobtrusively jot down any useful information which he may acquire.

He will pray for those he is about to visit before he sets out on his round, and he will do the same as he walks along the streets or stands at a door. 'So I prayed to the God of heaven, and I said unto the king.'[1]

During his visits he will be careful to let the people see that he comes to them as a man of God with a message from Him.

A young priest is often at a loss for suitable subjects of conversation. He will do well to aim at being a good listener and to get people to talk to him about their occupations and interests, and especially about their children ; he will usually find a ready response to his inquiries about these. He will be careful to

[1] Neh. ii. 4, 5.

discourage unfriendly gossip about neighbours, but will make a mental note of any information he may gather about them. His own attitude should be one of friendliness and sympathy, without, on the one hand, any suspicion of condescension and, on the other, any tendency to undue familiarity. Above all he should aim at being natural in his manner ; he will avoid undue self-consciousness if he constantly bears in mind that he is acting as the representative of the Master by whom he has been sent. Christian courtesy will prevent him from intruding upon the privacy of others at inconvenient hours, for instance, at meal times or at other times when his presence is obviously unwelcome. He should avoid giving the impression of being hurried, and, if he is pressed for time, should excuse himself and promise to come again when he has more leisure. Anything resembling favouritism should be studiously avoided. It may be pleasant for him to visit houses where he is assured of a hearty welcome, but if such houses are too frequently visited the fact will be noticed and may cause jealousies and heart-burnings in other directions.

In visiting those who are not connected with the Church it is inadvisable to begin by inviting them to come to church, for such invitations usually result in a ready promise to do so but without any real intention of fulfilment.

Some priests of experience seldom or never leave a house without asking permission to pray ; others, equally experienced, feel unable to do this in most cases without a sense of unreality. To the present writer the ability to end a visit with prayer appears to depend upon the personality of the priest and the opportunities afforded him. If it can be done quite naturally it is good to do it, and probably it could be done much more frequently than it is, for many people expect the clergyman to pray and are surprised and disappointed if he does not do so. But mere pious talk and any suspicion of unreality should be carefully avoided.

Care should also be taken not to confuse pastoral ministrations to the sick and to the whole with the administration of relief. If relief has to be administered to the needy and destitute it is better that it should be distributed through some lay agency rather than by the priest. This may entail a little more trouble at first, but it is well worth it.

In the first visitation of any parish or district it is well to visit every house, if possible, without distinction ; but on the following visits the priest will be able, and indeed will be obliged in any large parish, to exercise some discrimination. There will be families which are definitely attached to the congregation of some neighbouring church or who are practising Roman Catholics or Free Churchmen. It will be sufficient to visit these occasionally, say once or twice a year, in the absence of any urgent cause. Occasional visits create a friendly atmosphere. There will probably be some houses where the priest will meet with an unfriendly or even hostile reception. It is worth while revisiting these, for it is not at all uncommon to meet with an entirely different reception on subsequent visits, and some of the strongest adherents of the Church have been won by the tact and perseverance of the parish priest in dealing with what seemed at first to be quite unlikely material. Other families will be found to be already in touch with the Church in some way or other, and such will repay more constant visiting.

The great majority, however, will be found to be outwardly God-less, careless, and indifferent. In dealing with these, and indeed with all his parishioners, the priest will need to follow the example of His Master, by being on the watch for suitable opportunities to introduce the subject of religion, and by being quick to seize upon them when they occur. Births, deaths, marriages, some great joy or sorrow, or an accident, will open hearts to receive a message which have long been closed, and a priest who is in living touch with his people will be on the look-out for such opportunities and will recognize and use them. He should instruct his lay helpers, district visitors and others, to inform him of such occasions, and it is sometimes possible to find one of the faithful living in a street or court who will undertake to furnish the priest with such information without the source becoming known.

Mention has been made of district visitors. These should be carefully chosen, and should be taught that their main office is to serve as links between the clergy and their parishioners. They should be warned against any attitude of condescension, and if they are to be entrusted with any responsibility in the distribution of relief this should be carefully organized and safeguarded against abuse. Lay helpers may exercise a valuable spiritual influence, but this is almost inevitably weakened if they come to be regarded in the light of relieving officers. It is far better to place the distribution of relief in the hands of an independent committee, not necessarily confined to Churchmen, who have facilities for making careful investigation. Few things have done more to alienate decent, self-respecting working men from the Church than the indiscriminate relief administered to the undeserving, who have often made an assumption of piety in order to impose upon well-meaning clergy and visitors. District visitors should be encouraged to persevere in their duties by regular monthly or quarterly gatherings for prayer and intercession, to be followed by an opportunity of talking over their problems and difficulties with their priest.

If space allowed more might be said about dealing with special classes of people in the course of pastoral visitation. Managers of public houses and their families are too often neglected instead of being visited in the normal course. If the Church tends to regard certain classes as outside its pale they are apt to take the same view of themselves. Domestic servants form a class which does not always receive the attention it deserves. They should be visited and drafted into a local branch of the G.F.S., or into some guild where they can be brought under the influence of the priest and his helpers.

In many parishes men are seldom to be found at home during the afternoon, and certain evenings should, therefore, be kept free from meetings and organizations at which the priest is expected to be present, in order that he may devote the time to visiting the men. We lament the fact that we have not more men in our congregations ; may not this be largely due to the fact that the ordinary man has little or no opportunity of meeting the priest as a friend ? Too many priests allow themselves to become so immersed in parochial and other engagements that they have no time left for evening visiting.

When, owing to pressure of other work, the priest has little time for visiting, it is worth while that he should at least show himself in the streets of the parish.

A priest who is faithful in his visitation of the sick and the whole needs a strong sense of vocation and of the continual guidance of the Holy Spirit. He also needs much patience and courage, together with a sympathy which will render him wise and tactful, 'the tenderness which when wed with manliness maketh the man.' As has already been said of him in speaking of his ministry to the sick, he needs to be a man of God, a man of prayer.

'Who,' it may be asked, 'is equal to all this ?' 'Not one.' Each priest may, however, 'give diligence to show himself approved unto God, a workman that needeth not to be ashamed.' If the responsibility of the pastoral office is great and the disappointments keen, it has also its own peculiar privileges. 'Dulce est periculum Deum sequi.' There is the sweetness of being fellow-workers with God ; there is the joy experienced in the perseverance of the faithful ;[1] and there is the joy which is shared with the angels of God over one sinner that repenteth. The priest can thank God and take courage, for 'God's calling is God's enabling.'

[1] 3 S. John 4.

K

PENANCE : DISCIPLINE AND SACRAMENT

By Kenneth Escott Kirk

VI

PENANCE: DISCIPLINE AND SACRAMENT

THE CHURCH AND THE INDIVIDUAL

THERE is in common use a phrase, or pair of phrases, suggesting a theory of the Church's constitution which most Anglicans reject. The phrases seem to divide the Church into two parts—the *Ecclesia docens*, or ' teaching Church,' and the *Ecclesia discens*, or ' learning Church.' The ' teaching Church ' is constituted by the clergy, whose duty it is to proclaim what is to be believed ; the ' learning Church ' is composed of the faithful laity, of whom all that is required is that they should believe without question whatever is set before them authoritatively. History bears ample witness to the intellectual degradation which supervenes when such a theory is put into rigid practice.

But there is an opposite sense in which the two phrases might be used, which is far more congenial to much modern thought. In this sense the Church is conceived of as a kind of Extension Lecturer, giving popular information about Christian doctrine and Christian ethics,

but leaving it free to the listener to accept,
question, or reject. Her lecture rooms (on
this theory) are free to all who care to enter,
without distinction of creed, caste, or colour.
If they find edification in the instruction they
receive, no inquiry is made into their private
opinions ; the pew is not required to conform,
either in belief or in practice, to the principles
enunciated from the pulpit. 'Membership'
consists in attendance alone (and not always in
that), and so long as a listener is content to style
himself a ' member,' so long no other power,
no hierarchy, no authority, has the right to deny
him membership. To style oneself a member
of the Church of England, let us say, need mean
no more than to confess that on the whole one
prefers the type of religious *divertissement* staged
in Anglican places of worship to that provided
by Rome or Dissent.

Popular though this type of thought may
be, it is ludicrously unlike anything contained
in the New Testament. S. Paul would have
laughed at the suggestion that any Areopagite
who was pleased with his oratory on Mars' Hill,
and wished to hear more of it, might by that
fact avow himself a Christian. He numbered
his converts at Athens by name : Dionysius,
and Damaris, 'and others with them.' The
Church is a teaching body, no doubt ; but
it is of the essence of her constitution that she
shall teach not merely by the lips of her clergy,
but by the lives of her laity as well. And it

is to this feature of Churchmanship that Penance bears primary witness—to the fact that the lives of Christians must express the faith and ideals of their Church.

We are not merely so many sheep to be fed by our pastors. We are active members of a body dedicated to the proclamation in word of the means by which holiness is secured, but in deed—that is, in the lives of its members—to the illustration of holiness itself ; for which reason alone, if for no other, that body is rightly called the Body of Christ. Penance is the organic or administrative means by which this united and distinctive witness of Christian holiness is secured—just as preaching may be called the educative, and the Sacraments (including, of course, Penance in a second aspect) the operative means to the same end. We speak then, first, of the discipline of Penance ; and then of the Sacrament.

THE DISCIPLINE OF PENANCE

The discipline of Penance was in the early ages of the Church open and public ; the Prayer Book still calls this use of it a 'godly discipline,' and wishes that it might be 'restored again.' Notorious sinners, those whose lives palpably transgressed the Christian standard and therefore could no longer be cited or regarded as exemplary, were—not so much expelled from the Church as—segregated from the remainder, and placed in a separate category, until manifest repentance and contrition showed them to be fit for full membership again. In practice in some Christian bodies, in theory in all, this public discipline of the offender still continues ; but with that we are not concerned. For in the course of history a far more discerning institution grew up— that of private penance, or ' confession ' as it is more commonly called.

It was recognized that much which gave scandal and impaired the Church's witness could scarcely be dealt with by elaborate public processes ; recognized also, and with even greater discernment, that open sin has its roots in secret sinfulness, and that it is better to prevent scandal by eradicating its cause, than to cure it by lopping off its effects. And so Christians were urged (for they were never ' compelled,' except in so far as the appeal to loyalty and the pressure of public opinion constitute compulsion) to declare their spiritual state from time to time to the Church's representative, and from him to receive such correction, admonition, or reassurance as might be required, with the endorsement of their full membership of the communion if their contrition and promise of amendment (where contrition and amendment were necessary) seemed sincere.

This discipline of Penance, it will at once be seen, stands almost out of all relation to the question of a guilty conscience. Confession becomes an imperative duty, no doubt, to those who are burdened in conscience with grave sin. No one with even a shred of the sentiment of loyalty could deny that such a sinner, even though his sinfulness be known to himself alone, is bound in common honesty and fairness, if he wishes still to avail himself of the privileges of membership, to invite the Church to decide whether he still retains the right to those privileges ; or whether his condition is such as to make it necessary for her to refuse them to him until his heart change for the better. If we are right in thinking of the Church as a body whose witness to Christ is given not least of all by the overt conduct of her members, we can scarcely deny her an interest in their hidden spiritual dispositions also ; for the hidden character of the heart will sooner or later reveal itself in open action.

But the same submission of his spiritual state to the vision or supervision of the Church is, if not an imperative duty, at least a reasonable obligation upon the loyal Churchman who has no serious sin of which to accuse himself. Probably — most probably — there will be little that needs correction ; the matter is one verging upon a mere formality ; yet even so the Church, in the person of the confessor and others to whom the penitent makes known his practice of confession, will be rejoiced and strengthened by the example of loyalty thus given ; whilst the penitent will go away from

his confession secure in the conviction that he
has the approval of his Church upon his manner
of life and conduct. And once in a while it
may happen that one who thought that, despite
occasional lapses, his feet stood on firm ground,
will find in the process of his confession that he
is less safely placed in regard to sin and to
temptation than he supposed.

It will not necessarily be the case that he is
a man of hardened conscience. It may simply
be that a conscience, alert in most directions,
has overlooked an aspect of duty, neglected an
occasion of sin, or failed to penetrate to the
innermost cause of a moral weakness. In such
a case the discipline of Penance will suddenly
change in character. The Christian soldier,
who came to report himself watchful and to
inquire for further orders, will find himself
self-convinced of negligence ; and on the spot,
before the damage has gone far or deep, will
be able to promise amendment, and set himself
right with God and with his comrades in the
army of Christ.

Even then, if no sacramental character of
any kind were claimed for Penance, it would
still have an integral place in any scheme of
Churchmanship which tried to realize, to any
material extent, the New Testament conception
of the Church as the Body of Christ. Every
Christian, worthy or unworthy alike, would
by virtue of his loyalty alone be under some
such obligation of presenting himself from time

to time to the appointed representative of the
Body, to assure himself, and to be assured, that
his heart and behaviour were duly aligned with
that pattern of conduct which the Church has
undertaken by word and deed to set forth to
the world. There is nothing weak or effemin-
ate in recognizing such an obligation. The
best of us are liable to err in judgement ; the
strongest and most reliant may well desire the
fullness of corporate endorsement for their life.
It would be absurd to throw off the infallibility
of the letter of Scripture or the utterances
of popes, merely to enthrone the infallibility
of the individual judgement. Conscience is
supreme for conduct ; yet a conscience which
did not welcome opportunities of checking and
correcting its verdicts in the light of the verdicts of the community would stand confessed
as a conscience which claimed too much for
itself.

We have dwelt at some length upon this
aspect of Penance for two reasons. In the
first place, it is an aspect which should commend
itself even to those who cannot as yet admit
the sacramental character of confession and
absolution, but have no hesitation in facing
the obligations of loyalty. In the second
place, it explains a maxim of traditional moral
theology which has often proved a stumbling-
block to Anglican clergy—that the priest who
acts as confessor stands not merely in the
relations of father, physician, and director **to**

those who resort to him, but also in the relation of judge. It is his business to compare the spiritual condition revealed to him in confession with the standard of the Church as whose representative he acts ; and then, not in any private capacity but as the agent of the community, to absolve, admonish, or withhold absolution. Naturally enough, since it is almost always from among the ranks of the loyal and earnest-hearted that those who make their confessions are drawn, the refusal of absolution is a duty which falls rarely enough to the priest. But it is a duty which *may* fall to him at any time, which he must face, and for which he must prepare himself by study and by prayer ; remembering that by virtue of his office there is laid upon him the burden of judging as well as those of advising and of healing.

THE SACRAMENT OF PENANCE

We turn, then, to the doctrine of Penance as a Sacrament. One or two preliminary observations are necessary. It would be idle, in the first place, to attempt to vindicate its sacramental character to those who have no belief in Sacraments as a whole—in the doctrine that outward signs are means whereby we receive inward grace. It must be assumed that the reader is a sacramentalist, even though he doubts the sacramental virtue of Penance. And, secondly, it is not here proposed to discuss the question of the divine institution of Penance as a Sacrament, for the simple reason that it is unimaginable that our Lord should have required His people ever to accept any institution on the mere ground of His fiat. He appealed to obedience, it is true, but to an obedience enlightened by the understanding and warmed by the heart. We need not doubt that He gave the power to bind and loose to His Church, and that it is in accordance with His will that the Church has exercised or still exercises it ; but we have even so to use such understanding as is given us to bring that fact into harmonious relation with the whole scheme of Christian truth.

Again, let it be said that it is *only* with Penance as a Sacrament—as ministering and mediating forgiveness to the sinner—that we are here concerned. Many other benefits of a spiritual character are embraced in the purview of sacramental confession and absolution:—the self-knowledge which comes from examination of conscience, the relief of making a ' clean breast of it,' the help of godly advice and direction, and so forth ; benefits so great and obvious that from time to time they have obscured the central sacramental gift of absolution. So in the early days of the Oxford Movement, as Dr. Pusey attested, ' the practice of confession was revived, while scarce a word was said about absolution.' It is of the character of absolution in itself, however, not of the psychological value of confessing one's sins or receiving good advice, that we are here to speak.

With these preliminary observations in our minds, we may confine ourselves to two simple questions : (1) Is it reasonable that the forgiveness of sins should be mediated to the Christian through a sacrament ? and (2) Is it more reasonable that it should be mediated in this way rather than in any other ?

(1) It is of the essence of all true sacramental teaching that the due performance of a Sacrament does not evoke from God characteristics hitherto inoperative or gifts not hitherto bestowed, but rather focusses upon the needs of the Christian a spiritual benefit already and eternally present. If we think of the Incarnation and the Cross as the greatest of the Sacraments of God, it is not because we think that in them or because of them the divine love and the divine compassion first came into existence, but rather that in them the eternal love and compassion of the Godhead were specially focussed into visible form for human apprehension and acceptance. If we speak of a Real Presence of Christ in the Eucharist, it is not because we think that apart from the Eucharist He is really absent or unreally present; His Presence in the Eucharist is not so much *more Real* than elsewhere, as *more Realizable* [1] for man.

[1] By this phrase is not implied that the effect of a Sacrament is limited by the degree to which its operation is

How these things come to be is a part of that general sacramental doctrine which we have already agreed to assume as granted. But the principle holds good of Penance. There is an eternal forgiveness of God stretching itself out to men, enfolding them, cleansing them, welcoming them anew ; it is not claimed that the pronunciation of the words of absolution first calls it into being, or adds one jot or tittle to its efficacy. What it adds is just *realizability* ; it focusses the eternal and unchanging forgiveness of God upon the particular sins which the particular penitent has confessed.

Once again, we do not ask why an accredited minister of the Church—and he alone—should be the agent employed : that question belongs

consciously realized by the recipient ; otherwise Infant Baptism would be unjustifiable. Realization, or assimilation, can be unconscious and even inadvertent, as when a parent's bad influence is assimilated by, or realized in, his child's deterioration without any conscious imitation or co-operation on the part of the child. This question, however, important though it is, belongs also to the province of general sacramental theory. It is enough here to notice the point. At the same time, it is of the nature of the Christian Sacraments (thus differentiating them from pagan rites) that the 'sign' should bear some *intelligible relationship* to the thing signified—i.e. should stimulate the mind to thoughts, the heart to emotions, and the will to resolutions connected with the particular aspect of grace received. The 'sign' is *appropriate* to the thing signified ; it *speaks of it* as well as mediating it. This is obvious of Baptism and the Eucharist ; it is equally obvious that a solemn declaration of forgiveness is no less appropriate as the 'sign' of the divine forgiveness.

to the general question of the Sacraments, and presses no less in the matter of the Eucharist than in the matter of Penance. Nor do we ask why the formula ' I absolve thee ' should be the chosen means ; it is obvious that no other means could be more appropriate. We merely assert that if it is reasonable to think of the Eucharist as focussing the self-communication of God to man at a particular spot and time for particular communicants, so also it is reasonable to think of absolution as focussing the forgiveness of God at a particular spot and time upon the particular sins of individual sinners.

(2) But is it *more reasonable* that the forgiveness of God should be focussed in this way than any other ? Or, to put the question in another form, is the most reasonable course for any Christian who desires the continual forgiveness of God for his recurring sin to have recourse to this Sacrament ? May he not say, ' Repentance and silent confession in my own chamber is all that is needed—I can rest sure of forgiveness on those terms ' ?

Here again our reply must run along the lines of general sacramental theory, and the analogy of the Eucharist comes in once more. God is not tied to His Sacraments, of course ; but would it be reasonable for a Christian to say, ' I am so conscious of the abiding presence of Christ that I see no need to have recourse to the Eucharist for spiritual sustenance ' ?

The truth is, that some gifts of God are so vital and essential to the Christian, that only folly, pride, or insensibility could induce a man to omit any obvious and reasonable means of bringing himself more fully into the sphere of their operation. The presence of Christ is one of them—hence the attitude of the Christian who values that presence but will not receive Holy Communion is almost unintelligible. The grace of the Spirit is another—hence, also, the Church's insistence upon Confirmation. Is not the forgiveness of sin a third ?

The world is impatient enough at the Christian insistence upon sin. It prefers to forget its sinfulness, rather than to have its sins forgiven ; it is for this reason perhaps that many who have no hesitations about the Eucharist are genuinely puzzled as to the need for Penance. But Christianity has a different scale of values. It sees sin, even in its slightest forms, as an intolerable blot upon Nature and an overweening affront to God. So it is to the Christian, or to the man who takes the Christian view of sin, that the Church appeals. If sin is in any way that which the Bible represents it to be, can any means be superfluous which will make more real to the Christian the divine forgiveness of the sin which he deplores ? And if the sacramental factor in religion is (as Churchmen at least believe) of primary importance, surely that means which makes real the forgiveness of God *sacramentally* to the soul, by the

L

employment of an external sign ritually administered by the appointed representative of Christ's Church, is of all others the means which least of all can be regarded as unreasonable, negligible, or nugatory.

CONCLUSION

Considerations such as these will not bring men and women to their confessions, any more than argument will convert them or make of them communicants. The sense of sin, and the evidence of grace received by those who use the Sacrament of Penance, are the only motives strong enough to overcome our natural repugnance to so humiliating a step. But what has been said may be of some use in answering questions which arise spontaneously even in the most Christian minds.

If it be asked, 'Why should I make my confession?' the answer is, 'If for no other reason, because loyalty to the Church demands that you should assure yourself that her considered approval rests on your behaviour.' If it be said, 'But can a priest forgive my sins?' the answer is, 'No; but he acts as the agent of the forgiving Spirit of God working through the Church; in this Sacrament his function is neither more nor less than in all other Sacraments.' If a man urge, 'Surely silent confession to God is enough, for He is always ready to forgive?' we reply, 'Forgiving indeed He always is; but that does not exempt us from using *every* means by which we can appropriate His forgiveness to ourselves—least of all a means which, like the Creation, the Incarnation, the Cross, the Church, the Eucharist, is sacramental in character.'

Two things are lacking in the age in which we live—a sense of sin and a sense of Sacraments. It is for this reason that the questions just raised, and others akin to them, are pressed home so continually. But if we search unremittingly for ever better and fuller answers to the questions, never flagging in the attempt to make the practice of confession and absolution intelligible, we shall not merely reassure earnest Christians on points of difficulty. We shall also, little by little, restore an intellectual atmosphere in which both sin and Sacraments are estimated by the minds of men in their true proportions. And the more they are so estimated by the mind, the more also will they be truly apprehended by the heart ; the easier therefore will it become for men to turn, with mind and heart alike, from sin, and to seek the grace and goodness of God which lie in the Sacraments.

SPIRITUAL DIRECTION

By Henry Lucius Moultrie Cary, S.S.J.E.

VII

SPIRITUAL DIRECTION

AMONG the many cares and preoccupations
that claim the attention of the priest in
his ministerial life, there can be few to rival in
urgency and vital importance the duty and
privilege of satisfying and guiding the best
devotion of those committed to his charge.
Underlying the fervour of evangelistic and
missionary energy, is the zeal for the sanctification of those individual lives that give evidence
of a responsive quickening of their spirits under
the influence of the Holy Spirit of God, and
would transcend the claims of duty in yielding
to the attraction of Divine Love.

Yet, despite his consciousness of this demand
and his own loyal desire to meet it, he may not
infrequently be made aware of a certain restlessness or strain among those who are accounted
among the most faithful, a restlessness caused
either by their own sense of the meagreness
(as it seems to them) of the devotion round
about them, or by the taunts of critics who point
to the imposing lists of saints and *beati* of a
communion from which we are still unhappily
estranged, and ask what we can show to match

these signs of personal holiness and supernatural life.

By these and other kindred reflections we
are driven to realize that notwithstanding all
the ceaseless output of energy, and all the
inspiring self-devotion that have marked the
many years of the Catholic Revival, the general
level of spirituality, despite a few more or less
brilliant exceptions, is not really a high one.
The *sense of vocation* is not widespread, nor are
its claims, when keenly felt by the individual,
usually recognized, understood, and respected
by the generality ; and where devotional life
is rich and exuberant, it is all too commonly
apt to be found wanting in vital force and
stamina. After many years of the revival of
Religious Life, it is only quite recently that
any real attempt has been made to restore the
original idea of monastic devotion in the foundation of congregations consecrated to prayer
and penitence in what is commonly known as
the Contemplative Life.

These instances are adduced merely as
examples—as illustrative of the suggestion that
despite all the devotion of our faithful clergy
there may still be a failure to develop the
element of the truest spirituality ; and that this
failure means the waste of a dynamic force
which, if only it could be turned to full account,
would add immensely to the spiritual vitality
and to the sanctification of the Church. If we
suffer, and suffer lamentably, for the sins and

unfaithfulnesses, the doctrinal ignorance and aberrations, the tepidity and worldliness, of the vast number of those who claim membership with us, would not the intensification of spiritual life, and the training of those who are led to seek it in the Way of Perfection, be a mighty force to counteract these elements of our distress ? Has it ceased to be true that ' a little leaven leaveneth the whole lump ' ?

In view of a question so eminently practical, the subject of the scope and method of Spiritual Direction as a matter for consideration is brought forward in the hope that a better understanding of its meaning and value may lead to an appreciation of its importance as a means of contributing to the essential life, not only of a few isolated and favoured persons, but of the whole body of the faithful.

THE DUTIES OF THE DIRECTOR

It may be well at the outset to discriminate between the ordinary ministry of the confessional where normally a few words or sentences of counsel or instruction are given to the penitent, and this other discipline of direction which represents S. Gregory's *Ars artium*. Perhaps the distinction may be sufficiently clearly indicated by a quotation from a great French director of our own day, Mgr. D'Hulst. He says in a letter: ' There are obligations of conscience and obligations of heart. The difference between the good and the best concerns the latter obligations. This difference is needed to give play to love, for love takes its pleasure in doing *more* than the good—in seeking the best. If the best were a duty, love would have no margin left for its excesses. At the tribunal of penance, the confessor only judges of sin against duty. The director enters into the views of the Bridegroom, and grieves with Him about acts which are contrary to the finer sense of love. But he must not command where Jesus Himself is satisfied with attracting.' [1]

It would be superfluous to attempt to enumerate the doctors and teachers of the spiritual life, from S. Augustine, S. Gregory, John Cassian, or S. Bernard, down to S. Teresa and S. John of the Cross and S. Francis de Sales, who have emphatically declared and urged the imperative need of external guidance for those who are called to seek the Way of Perfection. A single quotation from a Spanish master may suffice to illustrate the traditional conception of this necessity, while it lays stress upon the loss to the general well-being of the Church of which mention has been already made.

' Of a thousand persons whom God calls,' he writes, ' scarcely ten respond ; and of a hundred whom God calls to Contemplation, ninety-nine are found wanting. For that reason I say " many are called but few are chosen." Instead of exaggerating the difficulties of this undertaking, and of falling back

[1] D'Hulst, *Way of the Heart*, i. 147.

upon the weakness of our nature, we must recognize that one of the main causes is the lack of spiritual masters. Woe to those communities who are without them, or who possess them, but fail to recognize or to value them.' [1]

We may say that Godinez writes in the interests of a very advanced spirituality, but even if we are reluctant to go so far as he would lead us, we must at least recognize that there are many degrees of mystical development, and that the elements of the mystical life are discernible in some stage or other in a very great number of souls.[2] Where these are in evidence, they are certainly not to be neglected, but should rather be regarded as of primary importance and deserving careful cultivation, if it were only for the sake of the soul of whose whole experience this must needs be an integral and highly formative part.

It is then at this point that the consideration of spiritual direction as we are now treating of it comes before us. We realize that there is a gift of God implanted in the soul ; how is it to be raised to its highest power, and made a principle of extensive sanctification in and for the Church ? How is it to be protected from

[1] Godinez, *Praxis Theol. Myst.*, lib. 8, cap. 1.
[2] The question of the universality of the call to divine contemplation is much discussed in current French and Spanish treatises of ascetical and mystical theology.

the innumerable dangers to which, by its very nature, it is exposed ? *Ars artium regimen animarum*—this is the task, the privilege, of the director of the spiritual life, the teacher of the Way of Perfection, the interpreter of the mind and will of God.

It is not enough to recognize the wide variance in the degrees in which the mystical element, by which direct consciousness of God is perceived, is present to the soul. Account must also be taken of the fact which, whether it is regarded sympathetically or otherwise, is indubitably true, that for one reason or another, there has been of late, and is at the present time, a great wave of quickened interest in subjects directly or indirectly bearing on the mystical life.[1] In morbid and perverted forms it is seen in Spiritualism and its various congeners. In saner guise it is manifested in the great number of devout persons who come for help about their difficulties in prayer, and who read the many books, old and new, that are pouring from the Press. That such writers as Jacob Boehme and Mme Guyon should be reproduced in cheap pocket editions is significant ; that they should have a wider vogue than S. Teresa or S. Francis de Sales is significant of danger. ' What,' we may ask ourselves, ' is likely to be

[1] It is sufficient to refer to the concluding paragraphs of the remarkable paper written by the late Vice-Chancellor of Liverpool, for the recent (1926) Church Congress, or the no less remarkable paper of Miss Evelyn Underhill.

the reaction to the stimulus afforded by such suggestion if the soul is left to guide itself ? ' The answer is found in every manual of ascetical or mystical theology. For our present need surely the reply should be, that it is as necessary that the *spiritual* danger should be counteracted by sound teaching and positive instruction, as that scepticism should be met with orthodox dogma and apologetic.

There is an ever present danger lest a soul under this stimulus may react in the direction of morbid self-consciousness, and become the victim of illusions, unless the priest who receives the confidence can, by his sound judgement, clear insight, and practical knowledge, make himself master of the situation, and establish an effective control for good. It surely is important that when a penitent or inquirer opens his need, he should be made to feel that though his statement may be (and probably will be) somewhat inarticulate and confused, yet that which is to him intensely real, should be immediately and intelligently apprehended and disentangled from the non-essentials, and that thenceforward there should be a line of development revealed to him along which he may, at the necessary inevitable cost, proceed towards the goal of life —the knowledge (ἐπίγνωσις) of God. To be met at this point with a blank disavowal of sympathy with the aspirations that are intensely real to himself, or to be put off with a faltering acknowledgement that the priest knows

nothing about such things, and with the suggestion that they are probably morbid or neurotic,
is to throw the soul back on itself, either to the
quenching of the Spirit of God, or to the very
morbidity of which it is implicitly accused.
Here should be found, rather, a note of clear
decision and the beginning of some positive
instruction which, even though it may of
necessity be elementary, may at least serve to
show where fuller help can be sought, and
where definite dangers and obstacles are to be
expected.   Here, as indeed throughout the
whole intercourse, pregnant suggestion is invaluable, as S. Ignatius in his second annotation
of the *Exercises* lays down : ' It is not abundance of knowledge that fills and satisfies the
soul, but the inward feeling and tasting of the
things ' (*el sentir y gustar de los cosas internamente*).

How wide the field of such inquiries may be
can easily be imagined. We may take as instances three subjects which are continually
being brought forward, representing what we
may perhaps count as essential and instinctive
attractions in the soul that has felt the presence
of God and the appeal of the Crucified.   *Mortification*, by which the soul would seek greater
detachment and purification from the tainting
influence of sense and desire. *Penance*, through
which the holy ambitions of the soul would
satisfy their longing to ' fill up what is behind
(ἀνταναπληρῶσαι τὰ ὑστερήματα) of the afflictions

of Christ.' And *Prayer*, which, taken in its simplest and most comprehensive sense, is a reaching out of the created soul of man after the knowledge and love of God.

None of these is negligible ; indeed, sooner or later, they will all appear as indispensable. None is without its dangers, none without its opportunities. But to know how to discriminate between the true and the fallacious, the temperate and profitable, and the excessive and perversive, this is the task of a discreet and experienced guide.

But if discretion is needed with respect to mortification and the discipline of penance, the necessity is urgent in the matter of prayer, and it is here that the development of spiritual and supernatural life is most in danger of arrest. Systematic mental prayer (usually in the way of discursive meditation) has been very widely taught and practised for many years ; but little account seems to be taken of the fact that the reasonable and logical result of perseverance in meditation is to bring the soul onwards to a purer and more immediate relationship to God in prayer, so that the mystical faculties, to which reference has already been made, tend to become liberated and enhanced, and with their growing ascendancy to encounter the difficulties and trials which are quite inevitable. For such exigences, the guidance and the decision of a competent director are of the greatest importance. Who but an outside critic, equipped with knowledge, and enlightened by the wisdom of the Spirit, can hope to discern with reasonable confidence the signs by which true progress can be recognized, by which the right and duty of forsaking an old and well-worn method (whose use has seemed to become impossible) for another which belongs to an advanced spirituality, can be ascertained ? Moreover, it is not only by interior attractions and facilities that these matters have to be adjusted. Reference must be had to the temperament ; and even the external conditions of the life have to be taken into account. No little harm may be done by the imposition of rules unsuited to the condition of the subject, or by lack of flexibility in the application of principles however well established.

DISCERNMENT OF SPIRITS

Before passing to the consideration of the director, and his qualifications for the office, it may be opportune to touch upon a subject already hinted at—the task that is normally known as the Discernment of Spirits. The importance of this is significantly brought out by the care devoted to the subject in the *Spiritual Exercises* of S. Ignatius, who gives fourteen rules for the discernment of spirits at the close of the first week, and eight more in the second week. The subject is developed more or less fully in most treatises on the spiritual life, and there is a monograph by the great Cistercian, Cardinal Bona, *De Discretione Spirituum*.[1]

Personal experience, however, is more likely to bring home the reality of the need than the treatises of the learned, and we are more concerned to know how the faculty is to be acquired than to demonstrate its utility. A very small experience of spiritual ministration will suffice to demonstrate the value of a discrimination which can discern the true origin of the motives from which the phenomena of the soul's life are derived. The many graces of the spiritual life have their counterfeits whose origin is evil, and whose end, if their course is not checked, is disaster. On the other hand, experience of discipline and trial through which the soul has to pass for its purification and refining are by no means to be treated as proof that the soul has been abandoned by God, or that it has strayed from the Way of Perfection.

The insight which will enable the director to discover the source and the values of the phenomena of the life that is submitted to his guidance will be among the most important of his qualifications. It is found sometimes in men of great personal holiness as a gift or charisma of the Spirit (it has been noticeably clear and strong, for instance, in the lives of such masters as S. Philip Neri and S. Francis

[1] Attention may be called to the invaluable edition of the *Exercises of S. Ignatius* with Commentary and Directory by W. H. Longridge, S.S.J.E.

M

de Sales), where its exercise will be apt to appear abnormal and even supernatural. But more normally it may be classified as a faculty developed by prayer, close study, and experience.

QUALIFICATION AND TRAINING

We must proceed now to what may be after all the most important part of our consideration —the question of the qualification and training of the priest himself to whom the ministry is entrusted ; premising—though perhaps the note is almost too obvious to need expression— that the qualifications, or at any rate those on which most stress is to be laid, are dependent largely upon growth and development ; so that although the ideal proposed may seem high and the standard exacting, yet there is reasonable hope that a priest of real devotion, if he would devote himself to the task, might make considerable progress through self-training towards this acquisition.

The three qualifications most commonly insisted on are those of Learning, Spirituality, and Experience. Let us try to see briefly what they severally mean.

Learning. Inasmuch as the task involved is that of leading the soul to direct knowledge of God and open intercourse with Him in obedience and prayer, it is obvious that wide and deep knowledge of the sacred Scriptures is of the first importance. By this is meant not so much an up-to-date acquaintance with the results of recent and current criticism, however essential that may be for the apologist and the teacher in other schools. The Way of the Interior Life is pre-eminently the way of the heart rather than of the intellect, though understanding must indeed bear its part in contributing to the knowledge by which love is to be kindled and enflamed. The sacred Scriptures should be read constantly, prayerfully, reflectively, until the mind is stored with instances and suggestions. The pages of S. Augustine, S. Bernard, S. John of the Cross, teem with illustrations and quotations—not always apposite or wholly just, as our more critical minds may sometimes urge—yet cogent as evidence that the written word was to them a living word, the 'lively oracles' of God. Every priest will remember how insistently in his own recitation of the divine office the words of the Psalter touch, quicken, and give expression to the otherwise inarticulate desires and aspirations of his heart. How often in the most familiar exercise of the ministry of penance and in instructions an instance from the holy Gospels or a pregnant phrase of S. Paul have carried more conviction than our own argument and exhortation. The language and the witness, the atmosphere of the sacred Scriptures, are among the most necessary resources at our command. Let us see that they *are* at our command.

Conjoined with this familiarity with Scripture there is needed a careful and accurate study of dogma as an indispensable means towards the discernment of spirits to which reference has already been made. If we are to ' try the spirits whether they are of God,' then we have the canon laid down by S. John [1] to guide us, and we should know the doctrine of the Incarnation as fundamental, and all that we can learn of Christian dogma as dependent on and explanatory of it, if we are to apply the criterion of truth. We need only—to take an obvious example—recall the antagonism between Christian Science, Spiritualism, Higher Thought, and some of the many modern forms of so-called Mysticism, and the Catholic Faith, to understand the uncompromising attitude of repudiation that the Church, where she teaches with authority, takes with regard to these movements and ideas.

So far the requisites are among those necessary to the priest in all his work for souls, whether in the tribunal or in instructions on the conduct of the common Christian life. With the beginning of this constructive work in formative training there comes a further need.

Ascetic. The storehouse of the Church is rich in the recorded experience and teaching of those doctors and interpreters who in their generation have helped forward in the way of sanctification the disciples and pupils who have

[1] S. John iv. 1, 2.

looked to them for guidance. The science of
the saints, like every other science, has its
text-books, its manuals, its treatises, dealing
primarily with the ordinary practice of self-
discipline and spiritual edification. These form
the library of ascetical theology, and they em-
body a tradition which may not be ignored.
The counsels and precepts will be found to
vary in the insistence laid on details, in accordance with the spirit and needs of the era of the
individual author, and may be representative
of some particular school to which he belongs;
but the underlying principles are constant, and
the main objects are the same, for all are concerned with Christian perfection, its degrees
and its practice, the obstacles that have to be
encountered, and the means available for the
enterprise, such as self-knowledge, mortification, and prayer. With such themes as these
the writings of the fathers and doctors and
teachers of the Church have been concerned all
through the Christian age. The very wealth
of material supplied, and the changing spirit
of social life, have caused the compression of
the teaching of the earlier masters into the
briefer treatises of modern times ; but a
Surin, a Lallemant, a Guilloré, a Scaramelli,
are the heirs and successors of those masters;
and if we have not time for the study of
S. Augustine, S. Basil, S. Gregory, and
S. Thomas, we can learn from them in the
pages of Grou, Tissot, Ribet, and a multitude

of others who have written for the needs of our own time.

Ascetical theology, then, may be taken, at least for our present purpose, to represent the science by which supernatural light is brought to bear upon the normal phenomena of the soul's life in its quest after perfection, and as such is invaluable to the priest who is called upon to guide.

Study of Man. But we shall do well if, instead of contenting ourselves with the study of specialized *Christian* moral science, we go further down to the study of man as man. The last quarter of a century has seen no small change in the relationship between faith and science, but there still remains an element of suspicion, and while scientific men have made great advances in the direction of sympathetic openness to suggestion, they are apt still to complain of the rigidity and intransigence of the Church and its teachers, and the complaint is not without some suspicion that the attitude is the result of ignorance and apathy. It is claimed that few of the sciences have made greater strides of late than psychology, and the result of the laboratory work of the last few years has appeared in the clinical psychology which has quite recently been making rapid development as a direct consequence of the War. Psychoanalysis, psycho-therapy, neurosis, are becoming almost household words, and there is a large literature, both technical and popular, growing up apace. It is surely in the highest degree desirable that this should be watched, and if possible used, inasmuch as the secular science represents the best work with proved results of some of the ablest students in that very field in which we are engaged as *Christian* practitioners—the spirit, soul, and mind of man.

Mystical Theology. Thus far, then, we have the study of the normal in the light of the supernatural in ascetic theology, and the study both of the normal and the abnormal in the natural light of psychology. There remains the study of the supranormal phenomena of the spiritual life in the light of the supernatural, which is the province of mystical theology. Let it be remembered that this science deals with the most intimate, vital, and difficult experiences of the life of the soul. How intimate and difficult for the ordinary student the study may be, those who have read carefully Baron von Hügel's monumental work on the *Mystical Element in Religion* will know. But in proportion to its intimacy, is its absorbing interest, and those who are called upon to discharge the duty of ministering to the finest and truest elements in the spiritual life of the Church and of the individual souls committed to their care from time to time, cannot afford to disregard its claims.

Here again the literature is extensive, though a very large part of that which is

available is rather academic than experiential.
That is to say, it represents the scientific work
of non-mystics in exposition and criticism of the
mystic.   There can be no doubt as to the
relative values of the two, though for most of
us the work of the exponent and the critic is
necessary for an intelligent use of the material
at our command.[1]   The catena of Christian
mystical writers from S. John and S. Paul
reaches down through Dionysius, the Fathers,
S. Bernard, and the Victorines to the Teutonic
School of Eckhardt, Tauler, Ruysbroek, and
Suso ;   the English School of Rolle, Julian,
Hilton, and the author of the *Divine Cloud* ;
and the Latin Schools of Italy and Spain which
attained their apogee in the great Carmelites
of the sixteenth century.   Its original contents
have been expounded and commented upon by
disciples and students such as Father Baker
and the eminent Jesuit teachers of the School
of Surin and Rigoleuc, and the Carmelites who
followed the Teresian Reform ; and the whole
has been again passed under review and the
results offered by such contemporary authors
as Père Poulain in his *Graces of Interior Prayer*,

[1] Father Vincent McNabb, O.P., writing of the visions
of great mystics, says : ' Such visions, whilst adding nothing
new to the deposit of faith, yet serve to give theology a new
image of divine things.   Hence it is advisable for the
theologian to rise from his S. Thomas or his Billuart to refresh
himself with the Dialogues of S. Catherine, or the *Interior
Castle* of S. Teresa.'

Abbé Sandreau, Père Lejeune, the Dominican
Fathers Arintero[1] and Garrigou-Lagrange,
Father Devine the Passionist, and Baron von
Hügel whose work, as we suggested just now,
stands apart from the rest in its wide erudition,
its familiarity with current philosophy, its penetrating and sympathetic insight, and its power
of exposition.

But if S. Teresa and others of the great
teachers set learning in the forefront, it is only
as first among qualifications that are needed for
the training and guidance of the soul.   Among
the maxims of S. John of the Cross are found
these pregnant sayings : ' It is not every one who
is fitted for the direction of souls ; it being a
matter of the last importance to give right or
wrong advice in so serious a matter as that.
(188.)

' The inclinations and tastes of the director
are easily impressed upon the penitent. (190.)

' However high the doctrine, adorned the
eloquence, sublime the style, the fruits of the
sermon will be in general no better than the
spirit of the preacher.'

To learning, therefore, must be added of
necessity a true spirituality of life. ' God is
angry,' says S. John naively, ' with those who
teach His law but keep it not, and who preach

[1] The *Evolucion Mistica* and *Cuestiones Misticas* of P.
Arintero are made specially interesting by their rich
documentation. Unfortunately they have not as yet been
translated from the Spanish.

spirituality to others without being spiritual themselves.'

We shall not be hindered from responding in a reverent, humble spirit to the demands made upon us for help and guidance, because we have not yet mastered all the science of ascetical and mystical theology ; nor shall we be deterred by the realization that we have not yet gained the heights of perfection which belong to real sanctity. But we ought at least to have laid secure foundations of reverence and piety, and to be engaged in the task of our own sanctification by all the means in our power. What kind of light will be gained from a priest who is only found at Mass when he is called upon to celebrate the mysteries, who seldom makes any attempt at meditation, and neglects his retreat ?

The Virtue of the Director

The worst kind of direction is that which seeks to impose the private ideas and methods of the priest upon the penitent, regardless of the light which the soul has already gained from God. The best is that which, as an echo of the divine voice, makes intelligible to the soul the purpose of the holy will already speaking within the depths of its being. The voice of the director is the echo of the Holy Spirit whose inner voice is a quickening life within.   Therefore the priest himself must be of necessity a man of prayer, not only for the sake of the experience from the resources of which he can teach and exemplify, but still more for the sake of the intuitive understanding of the ways of God, and of the selfless dependence upon the light of God which he is to receive before he can transmit it—which he must at least begin to know before he can teach it. It is only by the dependence upon God gained and matured in prayer, that he can be secure in the action and reaction of personalities one upon another, safe from the influence of affections and dislikes, attractions and repulsions, which, if indulged, would not only destroy all impartiality of judgement, but would also cloud and bedim the divine light. By such imperfections in his ministry he is in danger of bringing discredit upon the office that he is supposed to exercise solely and purely for the greater glory of God.

Of the spiritual habit of the ideal director of souls, Ribet in his invaluable *Ascétique Chrétienne* [1] says : ' The characteristic note of priestly piety which gathers up all the rest is a close union with God in the actions of everyday life, and most especially in this very exercise of direction. To direct his own soul aright and the souls of others, he has one rule only— that is God. He goes to God and he leads to God.'

And the same author says of the priest whose character bears this deep impress of personal holiness : ' When souls are able to recognize

[1] p. 387.

a true man of God, they hasten to him. They
are led and guided by a kind of instinct, and
this same interior attraction which calls them
to God calls them also to him who is to be to
them the organ of His will and the instrument
of His blessings.'

But if reverence and piety are fundamental
virtues needed for the discharge of this high
task, zeal is also required to quicken his energies. We have no need to be reminded of the
place that personal love for God must always
have in the life of the priest, nor of the charity
which, inspired by the love of God, finds expression in evangelical love for others, the
grand soif des âmes which relieves from tedium
the personal ministry that might otherwise be
so wearisome. But we may perhaps allow ourselves to add to these, as fruit and evidence of
holy zeal, the spirit of reparation, by which
from his own contemplation of the sacred
Passion and his own adoring sense of the
majesty of God, the priest is led to see, not in
his own life and labours only, but in the
spiritual life and conflict of others, opportunities for developing the fruits of holiness which
shall be to the glory and praise of God. If
God is glorious in His saints, if His majesty
is outraged by indifference, it is but the first
impulse of supernatural life that would inspire
us with a desire to make amends for that outrage
by training up a faithful and a holy Church
which should offer a continual sacrifice of

righteousness, and worship the Lord in the beauty of holiness.

But zeal must be balanced by a further virtue of prudence if the work of sanctification and reparation is not to be marred. Perfection indeed is the aim, but perfection has its degrees, and all cannot be measured by one common standard, or led by the same road. If we seek to hold the ideal of perfection before the eyes of the penitent, it must be a perfection appropriate to his state. There is a whole world of spiritual possibilities beyond the ken of the beginner, and with each stage of advance new vistas are revealed. Prudence will enable the guide to direct the aim, and concentrate the efforts along a way of continual progress, so that confidence and a disciplined spirit of enterprise will take the place of the rash, undisciplined adventures which are likely to lead only to disappointment and the dissipation of the forces of the soul.

There remains the third qualification of which we have spoken, that which will perhaps seem most difficult of attainment—experience. Experience may have two very different meanings, and in the first sense it seems as though it must be beyond our own control. For experience in its truest sense would mean that he who would guide must have himself already trodden the road, and known in himself the values of those experiences of the spiritual life with which he has to deal. Other things being equal, it is

clear that knowledge gained at first hand of the
trials, sufferings, and temptations of the soul
in its purification and stages of advance, will be
more convincing than theoretical knowledge
more or less tentatively applied. The priest
will teach how courage and steadfastness are
to be maintained in darkness and desolation,
if he has fought his own way through them.
He will be able to insist on perseverance, if he
himself has persevered. The piety of which
we have spoken may dispose the soul for the
receiving of the graces of interior prayer, but
it is of their essence that they are a matter of
vocation and gift and not of merit.

In the second, easier, sense, experience will
only mean that study and deep interest have
borne their fruit. Sympathetic observation,
with readiness to learn by mistakes, as well as
by any success that may have been attained,
have enriched the mind, and enlarged the outlook of the director, and provided him with
instances by which he can estimate the values
of those elements in the spiritual life of prayer
that lie still beyond his own actual degree.
As the student of moral theology reads his
' cases ' as well as his treatises, so the director
learns from his ' cases ' how his rules are to be
applied.

Conclusion

After what has been urged we may in conclusion return, and return with insistence, to

the suggestion that the whole subject has a very real bearing on one of the most vital needs of the day. The Church has need of the holiness, the fervour, the spirit of sacrifice, of which abundant evidence is not lacking, as living forces against the irreligion, the apathy, the hideous self-indulgence and worldliness of the age.

Nor may we allow ourselves to forget that a right proportion must be continually observed, and all obtrusion of self rigorously debarred. The Holy Spirit is the one Guide, and the director's concern is to teach and train the soul to listen for His voice, to hear its lightest whisper, and to obey its every command. That he may be enabled to fulfil this sacred and most delicate trust, he must set the cultivation of his own spiritual life before every other consideration, seek to learn the secrets of the discipline and the doctrine that he teaches, and to penetrate into the hidden places of the love of God by prayer.

PUBLIC WORSHIP

By Geoffrey Hare Clayton

VIII

PUBLIC WORSHIP

THE ALLEGED DECLINE IN CHURCH ATTENDANCE AND ITS REASONS

IT is generally believed that the number of people attending Public Worship in the Church of England is smaller to-day than it used to be. But there is not universal agreement about the facts. There is no doubt that it is much smaller than it ought to be. But some, who from their experience are not unqualified to form an opinion, maintain that, if the very great increase in the number of those who make their communion at an early hour is taken into consideration, there is no very marked decline. Certainly in the days when most churches had pew-rents, and in many churches there were not many free seats, the number of working people who went to church cannot have been very large. It is probably among the class of people who in old days did take pews that the decline in church attendance is most noticeable.

On the whole it would be true to say that attendance at church to-day means rather more than it used to mean. There are many parts

of the country in which to be a regular member
of a congregation is to be a marked man.   It is
no longer taken for granted, but is a definite
act of adhesion to the Christian religion, and
is understood to be so.   For a very long time
past the number of people who have desired
to commit themselves to a definite profession
of the Christian Faith has not been very large.
And the fact that church attendance is regarded
as such a committal of oneself no doubt
accounts for many people staying away from
church.   There is probably a more widespread
fear of hypocrisy, a more general desire for
sincerity, than in previous times, and this, which
in the main is a good thing, affects the numbers
attending church.

I say that in the main it is a good thing, but
the fear of hypocrisy may be carried to such
lengths that it becomes positively a bad thing.
When people are afraid to make any profession
of faith because they fear that they may not
always live consistently with that profession,
then they make a mistake. We must not refuse
to try for a good thing for fear lest we may not
always succeed.

Probably the fact is that the number of
people who are in vital communion with the
Church is as large as it used to be, but the
number of those who attend public worship as
a conventional act is smaller.   There are still
very large numbers of people who regard themselves as loosely attached to the Church—

evidence of that was given during the Great War by the religious classifications of the soldiers—but of these only a few attend on more than exceptional occasions at public worship.

We are thus confronted with a situation in which we find that the intensive work of the Church is prospering, and is increasingly absorbing the time and strength of the clergy; but that the impact of the Church on the outsider is getting less and less, and the opportunity of the clergy for getting into touch with the outsider is also diminishing.

Closely connected with this subject is the vexed question of Sunday observance. The great extension of opportunities for Sunday amusements, and the use that is made of these opportunities by people of every class, has revolutionized the English Sunday. Chaplains in the Army found often that men were willing to attend public worship, in order to ' pass the time,' as they frequently used to express it. And the same motive accounted for a great deal of church attendance in the past. Obviously to-day that motive no longer obtains to any extent. There are very many alternatives to church-going on Sundays. An increasingly large number of people find regular Sunday worship almost impossible owing to Sunday labour. And others can choose between many opportunities of amusement.

The Sunday labour which prevents public

worship is from our point of view an evil. The possibility of Sunday amusements is not altogether so. The Church is not taking up a very dignified position, if she opposes Sunday amusements on the ground that people will only worship God when they have nothing else to do. There are no doubt other aspects of this question, such as its effect upon the home life of the people, but with such things this essay is not concerned.

A considerable number of Church people would add another reason for the decline in church attendance. It is commonly said that the common substitution of the Mass for Morning Prayer as the Sunday morning service held at the time when most can be expected to be present is having its effect as a deterrent in keeping people from church. With regard to this matter it is very difficult to arrive at the truth. Those who take this line ignore the fact that in a very large number of parishes Morning Prayer is wretchedly attended. The general decay of conventional church-going has more effect on the attendance at Morning Prayer than at other services. And an increasing number of those who are in vital communion with the Church find Morning Prayer insufficient to satisfy their needs. This is especially true of the younger generation.

On the other hand, the enthusiastic Anglo-Catholic points to many churches where there is a crowded and devout congregation at Mass

on Sunday mornings. But he tends to forget
that most of the churches where this is so have
an eclectic congregation of people who come
from near and far to that church, because it
provides the services which they like. I would
not be thought to deprecate this in any way.
In the present state of the Church it is the
best thing that can happen. But it certainly
should be borne in mind, when we are considering the bearing of the nature of the Sunday morning service on attendance at public
worship.

There is no doubt that in the Church of
England to-day attendance at Mass does make
a greater demand upon people's spiritual attention than attendance at Morning Prayer, and
that, while this tends to bring the devout
Church people to the Mass rather than to
Morning Prayer, it has the opposite effect on
many of those who are but loosely attached to
the Church. There are many who feel comfortable at Morning Prayer, because they do
not feel that they are very seriously committed
to anything by attending it, but who feel uncomfortable at Mass, because its implications
seem to make demands upon them which they
are not prepared to satisfy. And so the tendency to substitute Mass for Morning Prayer
acts in the same direction as the other things
that have been mentioned, in strengthening the
intensive at the expense of the extensive work
of the Church.

The Obligation of Public Worship

Such are the conditions of the problem which we have to face. Can any suggestions be offered which may be of service to the parish priest in facing it ?

The first thing to be done is to realize that we have to try to get back the sense of obligation into the minds of our people with regard to their relation to God and His Church. At present their general attitude towards public worship is that they are willing to go when they feel inclined, and to a service from which they think they 'get some good.' It is our business to see to it that the services are such that they may be able to 'get some good' from them. But they are not very likely to do so as long as they go primarily with that intention. They must be taught about the duty of public worship, as being one of the duties involved in their religion.

It is not easy to teach them this. We have to contend with the general decay of the sense of obligation among our people, which shows itself in their relation to other matters besides their religion. And we are faced with particular difficulties of our own. What is their actual obligation as regards public worship ? We should say that it was the obligation of being present at the Lord's Service on the Lord's Day. That is what we tell them ; but they know perfectly well that if they were to ask the vicar of a neighbouring church he would tell them something quite different. And so many of them do not take us very seriously when we tell them of this. For they do not believe that we have any authority behind our words. We may be able to convince a few that we have the authority of the Church behind us, but many will not really believe this in the light of what they see around them. We must certainly persevere with this teaching, for we believe that it is true, and we shall convince a minority. In time that minority may become a majority. But in the meantime we must make it easy for them to fulfil this obligation by providing a Mass at the time in the morning at which they are likely to be able to come to church.

We must not be content to go on providing Morning Prayer as what seems to them the principal service of Sunday morning, while telling the young people to come to some other service. If we do that, they will certainly think that the obligation of attending the Lord's Service on the Lord's Day does not apply to grown-up people. We cannot ensure a consistent attitude on this question among the various churches in a district. We ought at any rate to be consistent about it ourselves.

The whole question of Sunday observance is a matter of great uncertainty among our people. Deeply ingrained in their minds is the idea of Sunday as the Sabbath. They think of it much more readily as a Day of Rest than as a Day of Worship. If we teach the children that it is a Day of Worship, but that there is no reason why they should not play games as well, we find that parents who never come to church are sincerely shocked. And yet we shall never even begin to get public opinion right unless we do boldly teach the children, and such adults as will listen to us, that Sunday is a Day of Worship before it is a Day of Rest; that the right way for them to keep Sunday is to hear Mass, and so far as possible rest from their ordinary work ; that, if they fail to do this, when they reasonably might, they are committing sin ; but that they are not committing sin if they enjoy themselves in other ways during the rest of the day.

Such teaching, if it is to sink in and to overcome hardened prejudice, must be continually given. It must be given in sermons, addresses, and in magazine articles, for it is really important that it should reach others besides the children and young people. But, after all, the greatest and most effective opportunity for teaching arises in connection with preparation for Confirmation. Mr. Harold Ellis, in a most valuable book called *Confirmation Interviews*, has emphasized the fact that the object of preparation for Confirmation should be the formation of religious habits rather than the imparting of information. And there is nothing to which the efforts of the teacher should be more definitely directed than the formation of a right habit of public worship.

The Sunday Morning Service

But it is time to consider the vexed question of Sunday morning worship. I have already given reasons for my belief that it will prove to be impossible to inculcate the duty of hearing Mass on Sundays so long as Morning Prayer is retained in the place of honour on Sunday mornings ; for even those young people whom we persuade to come to Mass at an earlier hour will perceive that we acquiesce in attendance at Morning Prayer as an adequate discharge of their religious duties by their elders. But the fact remains that there are considerable numbers of people, who are animated by a vague sense of goodwill towards the church to which they belong, who are willing to attend Morning Prayer, but who are not willing to go to Mass, because to do so seems to commit them to more than that to which they wish to be committed. These people are to be found chiefly in the upper middle class.

There are of course some, who are entitled to all possible respect, who conscientiously disapprove of non-communicating attendance at Mass. I do not think that these are very many, and I think that we must try to convince them that they are wrong. That battle is now more than half won.

But it is important that we should make up
our minds as to what is the purpose of Sunday
morning worship.   The supreme purpose is
the glory of God.   But the question is how
best to secure that end.   On the one hand we
may set ourselves to try to develop the spiritual
life of those who are in earnest about their
religion.   If that is our object we shall certainly
make our main service Eucharistic.   But if we
do so, we run the risk of losing others.   The
other object which we can, if we will, set before
ourselves, is to provide a form of service which
shall give the ordinary man and woman of goodwill what they think that they would like, in the
hope of teaching them by our sermons and in
other ways to desire something better.   If that
is our primary object, we shall probably retain
Morning Prayer.

There are, no doubt, many parishes where
this question hardly arises—parishes where the
Mass is now the traditional service for Sunday
morning, or new parishes where there is no
congregation accustomed to Morning Prayer
to be considered, and where the priest can
build from the beginning on lines that he
would like.   I am not considering such parishes
now, but rather the older parishes, which
form the great majority throughout the country.
In such parishes I believe that, in spite of the
difficulties which will arise, we must aim at
making the Mass, by whatever name we may
call it, the main service of Sunday morning.

It is quite true that we may lose both money and individual members of the congregation. But it is more important to provide a service which can adequately express the worship of those who are genuinely trying to make progress in their spiritual lives than to provide a service which the ordinary man can attend without feeling that any great demand is made on him by it. Such a man will never be converted at Morning Prayer.

We cannot treat our morning service as a mission service. The kind of person who attends it is not willing to be evangelized, and, if he were, Morning Prayer, with its cold and austere beauty, is hardly the instrument likely to be used for the purpose. S. Paul tells us that it is our duty to aim at such an atmosphere of worship in the congregation that the casual outsider, coming in, should be forced to his knees and to the admission that God is amongst us indeed. Is that more likely to happen at the Mass or at Morning Prayer ? There can be no doubt as to the answer. Experience seems to show that the attempt to build up a Catholic congregation by teaching given at Morning Prayer is not successful. There must be expression-work in education, and in religious education that expression-work must be Eucharistic worship.

We are led to the same conclusion if we approach the question from the side of Scripture. The Jews, as taught by God, held that

all true worship was sacrificial. It is true that
they held services in synagogues in various
places, but they felt that there was one place,
and one place only, where they could offer what
was worthy of the name of worship, and that
place was the Temple of Jerusalem, where alone
they could offer sacrifice. Our Lord in His
conversation with the Samaritan woman seems
to ratify this idea ; but He says that the time
is coming when the exclusive right of Jerusalem
will be at an end. Indeed a mark of the
Messianic age was to be that in every place
incense should be offered to God's Name and
a pure offering—that is to say, sacrificial worship. But for Christians there is only one
possible form of sacrificial worship, and that is
Eucharistic worship, the presentation before
God of a sacrifice acceptable and accepted.

There are two practical questions that remain
to be considered. The first is the Church's rule
of Fasting Communion, and the second is the
problem that confronts the single-handed priest.

If our great Eucharistic service is to be
held late in the morning, and if there are to
be many communicants at it, most of them
will not be fasting. Now there is no doubt
that Fasting Communion is a rule which has
Catholic authority, and, if we are going to
encourage general non-fasting Communions, we
are running directly counter to Catholic authority. I do not enter here into the question of
the possibility of dispensations. If that be

recognized, it will not meet the difficulty, so that it does not come within the scope of this essay. No dispensations could make allowable general non-fasting Communions. And, at this present period in the history of the Catholic revival, to disobey Catholic authority in this particular matter is a very serious thing. For, apart from other considerations, we have to remember that the effect of our Catholic teaching is to make people more familiar with the Blessed Sacrament, and to diminish that sense of reverent awe with which it is regarded by those who are untouched by the Catholic revival, and which so lamentably tends to keep them at a distance from it. To keep the rule of Fasting Communion is a healthy corrective to what might be a highly regrettable result of our teaching. It does help to prevent people from treating their communions lightly. One of the chief dangers to modern religion is the idea that we must make it attractive and easy. To ignore the rule of Fasting Communion is to succumb to this spirit, and that is disastrous.

If, then, there is to be a Eucharistic service late in the morning, we must discourage those people who are not fasting from making their communion at it. This can be done by teaching, and by insistence on the observance of the rubric in the Prayer Book which requires notice of intention to communicate. And, at the same time, we must persistently teach the duty of Communion, in order to guard against attendance at Mass being regarded as a substitute for Communion. This does not very frequently happen at the present time. But we have to watch lest there should be any tendency in that direction. And this means that we have to provide opportunities for Communion at an earlier hour. And that brings me to the other practical difficulty. How is a single-handed priest to arrange for this ?

To give Communion from the Reserved Sacrament is a means of providing for special cases. Probably for some cases it is the only means of providing, where a man's work makes it impossible for him to come with others. But it is not practicable as a general solution for our difficulty, and, indeed, it would be undesirable if used for other than exceptional cases. My conclusion is that, where there are sufficient clergy, there should be an early Mass for Communion as well as the late Mass. But where there is only one priest, it is very doubtful whether he ought to make himself responsible for this every Sunday. It may be possible for him to provide for it while he is young and in good health. But a time is likely to come when it will be an intolerable burden. Probably the best solution, where the Priest is single-handed, is a Sung Mass at an hour when people can communicate fasting, at some time between 9 and 10 a.m.

This might well be the only Mass of the day. But it is extremely doubtful whether it ought

to be followed by Morning Prayer with full
choir. If it is, then Morning Prayer retains
its position in the minds of many as the principal service of Sunday. And that is what
must be avoided. It might be possible in
some places to arrange for Bible classes to be
held after the Sunday Mass ; if not, people
might be encouraged to amuse themselves for
the latter part of the morning.

Before I leave the question of Sunday morning I should like to add two things by way of
explanation. It is not suggested that a priest
coming to a new parish can or should in every
case change the services in this way at once.
What is suggested is that he should have an
objective about public worship. His objective
should be to bring as many of his people as
possible to Eucharistic worship every Sunday,
both because they will be fulfilling their obligation by coming, and because by that means they
will best learn to worship God in spirit and in
truth. And the plan that has been outlined
seems to be the best road to the attainment of
this objective.

I should like to add that I have not thought
it necessary to try to justify non-communicating
attendance. There are a good many people
who still feel a difficulty about it. That difficulty
can of course be met, and must be met, by
patient teaching. But this essay seems hardly
the place to outline a defence which must be
primarily theological.

O

Sunday Evening Worship

If the Sunday morning worship in a parish is to be of such a nature that it will minister to the intensive rather than to the extensive work of the Church—and that seems to be inevitable and right—great care must be taken that provision is made also for those who can at best be described as loose adherents to the Church. For it is nothing short of disastrous if all those who are nominal Church people, but really largely unattached, are not brought to worship at all, or are driven to Nonconformity. Therefore Sunday evening ought to be devoted to this extensive work.

It is very doubtful indeed whether an ornate Solemn Evensong is suitable for this purpose. No doubt it is acceptable to the faithful. But by the unfaithful it is not understood. It is at least equally doubtful whether in England, at present, 'Devotions' form a satisfactory substitute. They also are appreciated mainly by the faithful, and not understood in the least by any one else. Probably in most parishes the best form of evening service is a simple popular Evensong. The priest's own affection for Plainsong must not lead him to suppose that the unfaithful for whom he wants to cater will find it as helpful as he does. To most of them it seems a strange and outlandish thing. Moreover, it is important that we should remember that our main business is not to educate the musical taste of the people. If we can do so, so much the better ; but it must not be done at the expense of other things.

Probably an old-fashioned popular Evensong is in most parishes the best kind of mission service. It is true that, if we had to begin at the beginning, we should not use a choir office, with its psalms and lessons, for this purpose. But it is familiar to people, and is immeasurably more suitable for its purpose than most of the attempted substitutes for it. Great freedom may rightly be used in what is done after the Third Collect. The opportunity might be taken to give a good deal of practical instruction by example in simple prayers and intercessions. And of course the sermon is important.

It is too often forgotten that there are still in all classes considerable numbers of people who go to church with the one idea and hope that they may hear in the sermon some words which may stick in their minds and help them and encourage them through the dull routine of the week. That may show an inadequate idea of religion, but it is worthy of respect. Sermons on Sunday evenings may rightly be largely instructional in nature, but it is of great importance that the instruction should be brought into close relation with daily life, and that the speaker should not seem to be employing a language and following a train of thought which has no point of contact with his

hearers.   But preaching is dealt with elsewhere in this volume.

Our Objective

Finally let us get clear our objective.   What
is it which we hope to do for our people by the
opportunities of fuller worship which we provide for them ?   Public worship is not an end
in itself.   That they should obey the regulations
of the Church and fulfil their obligations is not
an end in itself.   Our objective is to bring
as many as possible into vital relation to our
Lord, and to keep them therein.   So we cannot
be content merely to provide the most attractive
kind of service.   We have to consider also what
the service is likely to do for them when they
have been attracted to it.

Thus in the ordering of our services we are
continually faced with the difficulty of considering at the same time the edification of the
faithful, the instruction of the ignorant, and the
attraction of the outsider.   There will be some
of these three classes at most of the services in
our churches.   In this essay it has been urged
that greater attention should be given to the
faithful on Sunday morning and to the outsider
or ignorant on Sunday evening.   But at all
services we have to remember the existence of
all three classes.   Our Sunday Eucharist must
be such that the outsider may be caught up into
an atmosphere of worship, and that the ignorant
may not be wholly unable to follow it.   Our

popular Evensong must be conducted with such reverence and care that the faithful as well as the unfaithful may find it an opportunity for prayer.

Perhaps one of the means of bringing this about is that the priest should himself remember that what has been said about public worship having for its end the bringing of people into vital relation to our Lord applies to himself as well as to his congregation. Great harm is often done by the apparent professionalism of the officiating minister. The man who remembers that in all his conduct of public worship, whether the congregation be large or small, he is representing the whole Church in its approach to its Lord, will in time infect his choir and his people with something of his own spirit of reverence. And, if he has done that, he has more than half won the battle. For, whatever be the motive for which people come to church, what the priest must set himself to do is to make them feel, when they are there, that they have come into touch with spiritual forces, that there is something going on which has to do with the spiritual world. So, and only so, will the public worship of our churches be a factor in converting souls to God.

THE HOLY COMMUNION

By James Buchanan Seaton

IX

THE HOLY COMMUNION

THE scope of this article will be limited in general by the purpose of the whole volume and in particular by the subject of the previous article. Obviously the doctrinal significance of the Holy Communion cannot and ought not to be entirely avoided, but there will be no full discussion of the doctrine. Again, the position which the Holy Communion should occupy in the parochial arrangement of services, though it may be implied in what is written here, is more properly dealt with by the article on 'Public Worship.' This article will attempt to deal with the Holy Communion from the pastoral point of view.

THE PRIEST'S DUTY

'Feed My sheep' was the charge of the risen Lord, and His word still lives in the charge delivered at the Ordination of a priest 'to feed and provide for the Lord's family.' The priest's duty is 'to give the household their portion of food in due season.' [1] It is his business to teach the necessity of the sacred Food, to awaken and renew the desire for it,

[1] S. Luke xii. 42.

to prepare for its due reception, to interpret its meaning, to draw out its connection with the Christian life until his flock come, so far as is possible for one congregation only, ' to a full-grown man, to the measure of the fullness of Christ.' [1]

WORD AND SACRAMENTS

The Holy Communion is not the only spiritual food which the priest has to administer : there are two tables from which the soul is fed, the Word of God and the Sacrament of Christ's Body and Blood. We are the ministers of both Word and Sacraments. Neither should be too sharply isolated, for neither is fully effective without the other. In the recovery of sacramental truth and privileges at one period of the Catholic revival, there was a considerable neglect of the study of the Word. But, as it has well been said, ' we should not always be living in reactions.' Our teaching about the Holy Communion should always go hand in hand with definite training in meditation or the devotional study of the Scriptures. ' The stronger your faith in sacramental grace, the devouter your approach to the Sacraments, the greater your need of the constant enlightenment which comes from the Word of God appropriated and absorbed by the mind and heart and will.' [2]

[1] Eph. iv. 13.
[2] Dr. Gore's Introduction to *Via Veritatis*, notes for daily Bible reading. (Longmans, 1913.)

One of the duties most pressing on the clergy of to-day is the duty of teaching their people, in however simple a way, to feed on the Scriptures which make men wise unto salvation. For only so can their thought be sustained at the Christian level and can sacramental grace be given its true direction. The efficacy of sacramental grace largely depends upon the constant renewing of the mind by contact with the mind of Christ. A young priest told the writer lately that he ended his Bible class for working lads with a short conducted meditation, the object of which was to bring them into personal touch with our Lord, receptive of His word. The result had been, as might be expected, a much richer experience in their acts of Communion.

That is just an example from ordinary modern parish life of the application of the principle. More will be said on this subject when we come to the preparation of communicants, but so much it was necessary to say at this point. For our whole treatment of the Holy Communion from the pastoral point of view should be inclusive and not isolated. It is not merely a particularly sacred religious act standing alone without connections. It should be made the focus of the whole moral and spiritual life of Christian people, not as individuals merely, but as members of the Body of Christ ; every act of devotion, by way of prayer or penitence or Bible study, should prepare for it or should be quickened by it ; every part of the Christian Faith is called into play, every relationship of social life is affected, and the fullness of Christian living implied.

The memory of a criticism made by a good old-fashioned Churchman to a young curate in his first parish still sticks in the mind : ' You are making too much of the Holy Communion.' But we can't make too much of the Holy Communion in our parishes, if we do it in the right way, and if we do not isolate it from the rest of our teaching and practice. Of course a reference to it at the end of most sermons is less than no good—it is apt to do positive harm ; or again merely to induce people to come to Communion, as though they might thus fulfil the law, is not the same thing as the making of disciples. But the Holy Communion *must* be central in the life of our parishes, and in the lives of our people, because it is the satisfaction by a divinely appointed rite of man's age-long search for God ; it is God's definite ' Yea ' to our sense that somehow we were made for fellowship with Him and in Him with one another ; it is the appropriation by us of all that our Lord has done and is doing to make this fellowship possible. If S. John's declaration be true that ' our fellowship is with the Father and with His Son Jesus Christ,' [1] then the Holy Communion must stand at the centre of our pastoral work ' that our joy ' as

[1] 1 S. John i. 3.

priests ' may be fulfilled.' ' Of all the great religions of the world it is the Christian Church alone which is so far heir of all the ages as to fulfil the dumb, dim expectation of mankind: in it alone the sacramental meal commemorates by ordinance of its founder the divine sacrifice which is a propitiation for the sins of all mankind.' [1]

The training of communicants is the chief work of the Christian priesthood, and no other activity can take its place. How is it to be done ? The prescribed limits of this article permit only a brief discussion.

THE TRAINING OF CONFIRMATION CANDIDATES

The life of Communion should naturally be the end hoped and prepared for in Sunday School and Catechism. It is the objective of all the children of the Church. This does not mean that there are to be a great many allusions to the Holy Communion or elaborated lessons on it. The end should always be in the mind of the teacher, but the means are such graduated teaching as will concentrate the mind and the heart and will of the child upon the Person of our Lord, and will stimulate the desire for Communion with Him in the way of His own appointment. Children's Eucharists, apart from other considerations which justify them, are a

[1] F. B. Jevons, *Introduction to the History of Religion*, p. 415.

valuable appeal and preparation of interest and desire. Children should be trained towards Communion by the planting of 'seed-thoughts' in their mind. The discussion of mysteries is not for them.

> My father, who knew better than turn straight
> Learning's full flare on weak-eyed ignorance,
> Or, worse yet, leave weak eyes to grow sand-blind,
> Content with dullness and vacuity.[1]

'Milk for babes' is the Apostolic precept, but there must be the supply of milk, or the babes will starve. When the story of the Institution of the Blessed Sacrament is reached in its proper order, there are two ideas in it, and probably only two, which any child can understand—'Do this' and 'in remembrance of Me.' Here is an appeal to loyalty and to love. Nobody can grow in the understanding of the mystery unless they begin there: without loyalty and love there is no such thing as the communicant's life. If by our life and teaching we can make the Person of our Blessed Lord real and attractive and inspiring, and have planted at the right moments those two thoughts about the Holy Communion, and have taught them to assist at the service, we have done all that is really possible in the training of children towards Communion. They can only learn more, when the time comes, under the Spirit's guidance, by use of the Sacrament in the discipline of life's experience.

[1] R. Browning, 'Development.'

When the special preparation for Confirmation approaches three points seem to be important. (*a*) In our scheme of instruction we should be careful to see that our teaching about the Holy Communion is not of the nature of an after-thought or an anti-climax. The place given to the discussion of the Sacraments in the Church Catechism is a warning. It was added to the Catechism at a later date, and in the minds of children it stands there as a sort of extraneous and superfluous addition. Somehow in our scheme of instruction our teaching about the Sacraments ought to be woven more closely, and in due proportion, into our teaching about the life, death, resurrection, and ascension of our Lord, the work of the Holy Spirit in the Body of Christ and His members. The Catholic Faith should be presented as one whole so that it can be seen as such.

(*b*) This point is made with some diffidence because it conflicts with the practice of many priests, but with a strong conviction of its soundness. Actual practice is a much more potent teacher than verbal instruction. There should be practically no interval between Confirmation and first Communion. The frequent habit of making the act of Confirmation the great thing to be prepared for, with another interval for further instruction before Communion, has the psychological effect of depressing Communion into a less important position in the minds of the candidates. If we could give all our instruction before Confirmation and admit the candidates to Communion on the earliest possible Sunday after, we should present to their minds more vividly the fact that Communion is the great thing to be desired and that Confirmation is the last stage of preparation before admission to it.

(c) What are we going to teach about frequency of Communion ? Are we going to be satisfied with teaching once a month as the ideal, or with attaching a particular sanctity to the first Sunday of the month ? We shall return to the general subject later in the essay. The writer is convinced from his own experience that from the beginning we ought to teach our children the ideal of making their Communion every Sunday; that the Lord's own Service on the Lord's own Day to them ought to mean their renewal of their fellowship with Him by Communion. Week by week at least they need their Food for the journey of life. There was great value in the awe which made occasional acts of Communion after long and serious preparation the ideal. But the battle of life to-day and its problems and difficulties for the growing child are so acute that we should not hesitate to urge, under due conditions, the rule of weekly reception of the Food of Life. It is their best defence and their best hope of progress in the faith which overcomes the world.

COMMUNICANTS' GUILDS

The communicants in most parishes of any size need to be organized in a guild or fellowship. In the earlier days of the revival of a strong communicant life in our parishes, it was thought desirable to organize separate guilds or classes for adult men, adult women, girls, and boys, and to build up the spiritual life of each group separately. But, though the method met with success where it was well worked, plainly it is out of harmony with the corporate character of Church membership. That is the real objection to it. At the same time it tended to an excessive organization. It is absurd in modern life that men and women communicants should be treated separately. In the Church life of our day, the tendency is to work on the lives of communicants through one guild or fellowship or class (different parishes give it different names), with its regular meeting for prayer and instruction.

There is one exception to be made to the grouping of all communicants in the same fellowship. Boys should be dealt with in a separate group for several years after their confirmation. There is a period of years in which the adolescent boy markedly draws away from the larger corporate life, inclusive of adults and girls, and protects himself by association with a herd or gang of boys of his own age. If they come to church, they will prefer to come with

P

the rest of their set ; if they come to Communion, they will prefer to come with the friends
of their own age.   It would seem that the only
way, normally, to build up a body of boy
communicants in a parish is to associate them
together by themselves in a special group.   As
they grow up, they can be in due time trans-
ferred to the larger association of communicants.
But (except in those happy cases where the
religious tradition of his family is strong enough
to foster the growing boy's religious habits)
boys will best learn the habit of Communion
in their own group.   It has been said that ' the
gang instinct is almost a cry of the soul to be
influenced.'   Priests who have the necessary
gifts will find their happiest and most fruitful
work in capturing and training a group of lads
for the life of Communion, and so preparing
them to take later their full place in the corporate work and witness of the Church.

Necessary Elements in the Training of Communicants

This subject might provide material for a
whole book, and can be treated but scantily in
a short essay.   The ideal is suggested in the
Evangelist's statement that our Lord chose
twelve to be with Him and that He might then
send them forth to do His work.   There are
the spiritual needs of the individual communicant ; and there is the obligation of public
witness to our Lord.   Further, the needs of the

individual are met only because he is a member of the Church, and the Blessed Sacrament is a 'divine safeguard against individualism.' Our teaching should be full enough to include these ideas in due proportion. In detail there are points which seem in these days to merit special treatment.

(*a*) *The needs of the individual soul* are urgent. Most of us were probably brought to the Holy Communion through our sense of need. Our souls cried out for the living God, Who met us at the altar in Jesus our Lord. No teaching can appeal to men and women with their manifold needs which does not assure them that the needs of their own souls can be satisfied. Therefore the individual communicant requires individual preparation, and must be taught to prepare himself. Books of devotion tend to take this work too much off people's own hands ; and one of our people's great needs is the use of greater variety in their methods of preparation for Communion, that they should not be content with going through a regular form of self-examination, confession, and prayer such as we have in our books. It wears very thin sometimes.

To return to a suggestion made earlier in this essay, we ought to be able to commend and to teach a reflective method of preparation, so that there is always in the communicant something of deep expectation when he approaches to offer and receive. It is this kind of preparation which will save people from cheap and easy and ready-made views about the Sacrament, and from glib phrases in which there may be occasion for controversy but no nourishment. Meditation makes the soul grow to correspond with the largeness of the gift. For there is nothing which may contract so small or expand so large as the Eucharistic Gift. The pass-words of controversy tend to contract it and to dim its wonder ; but reflection nourishes and expands it. It should be reflection on our Lord's own words. In this way the two tables of Word and Sacrament may be made one.

Ought we not to recommend more than we do the constant life-long use *in this connection* of the passage of the Gospels which has been as much used and loved as any other, viz. the last discourse and prayer of our Lord in S. John xiv–xvii ? *In this connection*, because the passage contains the thoughts which filled our Lord's mind on the evening when He instituted the Sacrament, and the words of His discourse are the interpretation of the meaning of our Communion with Him, its privileges and its duties. A book called *Ideals of Holiness*, by the Rev. F. W. Drake, gives most valuable help in this reflective method of preparation for Communion.

(*b*) We need to teach much more thoroughly *the inherently social character of the Holy Communion*.

It is not only within the area of Protestantism that an over-individualistic way of thinking about religion has prevailed.

It prevailed also in the unreformed theology of the Reformation period and the subsequent epoch. There, too, the tendency was to regard the salvation of the individual as the main, or almost sole, object of religion. The same tendency dominated in the revival of the sacramental teaching in the Tractarian movement. But that movement restored to us the idea of the church. And what we now need is to let our thought of the church and of the sacraments recover its original social colouring, so that we may restore the conception of human brotherhood to its true and dominant place among Christian conceptions.[1]

Personal holiness of course is the best contribution which the individual can make to the life of the Church, but it must definitely be offered to the fellowship, as indeed it can only be maintained and acquired within the fellowship. It has been said that ' what the Spirit is revealed in the New Testament as perpetually doing is to make " saints " ; but you will never find the word " saint " occur in the singular. Invariably it is plural. Holiness in the proper sense can only grow in the family gathered round Jesus Christ,'[2] just as character can only be formed in fully expressed family relationships. No other conception of religion can hold up its head to-day in the modern world.

The world cries out for brotherhood and looks to the Christian Church for its expression. The communicants of every parish ought to let it be seen that they love one another. Otherwise the Church cannot be expected to impress the

[1] Gore, *Body of Christ*, appended note 21.
[2] H. R. Mackintosh, *The Divine Initiative*, p. 100.

world. There are still many communicants in many churches about whom Dr. Temple's words are not too strong : ' We say our own prayers and pay our respects to our own God : and then we come out again and go to our own homes, to eat our own meals. We do not concern ourselves with the people in the next pew, unless they sing out of tune, when we brace ourselves for the extreme measure of turning round to look at them.' [1]

The times demand that the principle should be further extended beyond the fellowship of our own separate congregation to the greater fellowship by whose life it exists. ' O pray for the peace of Jerusalem : they shall prosper that love thee.' Controversy still rages round the Sacrament of our Redemption and divides from one another the hearts of many who devoutly receive the same spiritual Food. Of course the cause of truth compels debate, but the debate should be conducted in the temper of a true communicant, as S. Paul expresses it : ' with all lowliness and meekness, with long-suffering, forbearing one another in love; giving diligence to keep the unity of the Spirit in the bond of peace.' [2]

It is the priest's duty to reconcile and to lead the communicants of his parish from all bitterness, and in times of controversy to the spirit which promotes the peace of the Church.

[1] *Foundations*, W. Temple, article ' The Church,' p. 358.
[2] Eph. iv. 2, 3.

Hooker's words are always worth remembering: ' I wish that men would more give themselves to meditate with silence what we have by the Sacrament and less to dispute of the manner how.' [1]

(c) *The Moral Obligation of Self-sacrifice.* There is probably little danger, as was once feared, that the effect of Catholic teaching will be the substitution of attendance at Mass for Communion. Catholic theology does not favour ' substitution ' theories, whether it be in the doctrine of the Atonement or in the doctrine of the Eucharist, which, in this matter, are closely inter-related. The history of sacrificial worship shows that Communion is its main object and its most essential element. The Christian Eucharist proclaims Christ's Sacrifice as the new and living way by which our fellowship with God is restored. We can only go to God through Christ, but we must also go with Him and in Him, and that means that the communicant is part of the offering. The consummation of the Eucharistic Offering is the act of Communion by which in Christ ' we offer and present ourselves, our souls and bodies, to be a reasonable, holy, and lively sacrifice unto God.' S. Augustine's comment on S. Paul's words is : ' This is the Christian Sacrifice ; the " many " become " one body in Christ " and it is this that the Church celebrates by means of the Sacrament of the Altar, familiar to the

Eccl. Pol. V. lxvii. 3.

faithful, where it is shown to her that in what she offers, she herself is offered.'

In the recovery of the sacrificial aspect of the Eucharist have we made enough of its moral implications to the communicant, have we stayed ourselves too much on the privileges and blessings of the free access to God secured at the expense of dwelling on the sacrificial life to which the communicant commits himself ?

> Sweet awful hour ! the only sound
> One gentle footstep gliding round,
> Offering by turns on Jesus' part
> The Cross to every hand and heart.[1]

The Church can only be a sacrificial Church when its communicants have learned that Communion commits them to sacrifice ; and only by becoming a sacrificial Church can it win the world.   S. Paul says that the business of the Christian ministry is ' to perfect the saints unto the work of ministering,' [2] i.e. to fit the saints out so that they shall be qualified to serve. Communicants are pledged to Christian service, and service in a world like ours means sacrifice. In *The Eucharistic Life*,[3] a little volume of addresses given by members of the Oxford Mission to Calcutta to the Syrian Christian

[1] John Keble, *Christian Year*, ' Holy Communion.'
[2] Eph. iv. 12.   The meaning of his words is obscured in the Authorized Version.
[3] Longmans, 1919.

Church in Malabar, occurs a passage well worth pondering :

Through the Eucharist the Sacrifice of Christ which is offered to God becomes extended, i.e. it embraces the sacrifice of more people. On Good Friday when Christ's Sacrifice became, as in a true sense it did, complete on the Cross, it was the offering of Christ Himself alone, and no other members of the race shared in it. But since the time that our Lord began to impart His ascended human life to His disciples until this day, His offering has included the offerings of more and more of His disciples who, through the power of His life, have been able to offer themselves whole-heartedly to God. . . . If we do not offer ourselves along with the sacrifice of Christ, then we are but trying to offer something that may do instead of our offering of ourselves, which is to defeat God's purpose for us.

In days when the world is crying aloud, from every quarter, in its need of Jesus Christ, ought we not to urge more fully upon the communicants in our parishes that their communion commits them to spend themselves in the cause of Christ ? God's missionary purpose depends upon the completeness of their self-oblation. A communicant who is not keen on the spread of the Gospel hardly has the right to partake of the altar. The ' World Call to the Church ' presented at S. Paul's-tide of 1926 has revealed the extent of the sacrifice required and the greatness of the God-given opportunity in our day and generation. Our communicants' guild or fellowship in the parish should become also its missionary society, instructed on the method of the new Missionary Schools

organized under the direction of the Missionary
Council of the Church Assembly. Somehow
the priest should help the communicants of his
parish to catch the meaning of the vision perceived by Marius the Epicurean at the Christian
mysteries.

Marius could discern dimly behind the solemn recitation
which followed, at once a narrative and a prayer, the most
touching image truly that had ever come within the scope
of his mental or physical gaze. It was the image of a young
man giving up voluntarily, one by one, for the greatest of all
ends, the greatest gifts ; actually parting with himself, above
all with the serenity, the divine serenity of his own soul.

FREQUENT COMMUNION

History shows that times of religious revival
are marked by an increase in the frequency of
Communion. It is impossible to speak too
definitely about the early practice of the Church;
it varied in different places and at different
times : whether daily Communion or weekly
Communion on the Lord's Day was the practice, in any case the rule was that Communion
should be frequent. A recent Roman Catholic
writer affirms that the whole cult of the Blessed
Sacrament was concentrated on Communion
until the thirteenth century.[1] Even after the
invasion of the Western lands of the Roman
Empire by the new nations, we have voices
raised urging even daily Communion upon the

[1] Ch. Cordonnier, *Le Culte du Saint Sacrament*, p. 73.
(Lethielleux, Paris.)

faithful. That can only have been in places where ordered life continued or where it had been rebuilt.[1] But the habit declined, at least through Western Christendom in the middle of the ninth century, and until the Reformation Communion became quite infrequent. The Lateran Council of 1215 could not require it more than once a year of the laity. S. Louis only communicated six times a year, and that was regarded, said the Benedictine writer, in his age as frequent Communion.

With the revival in our own Church and in the Roman Catholic Church in the sixteenth century it was natural that the minds of the faithful should be turned to their neglected privilege. The English Prayer Book of 1549 contemplated weekly Communion at least, though the minimum requirement in 1552 was thrice a year, in itself an advance on the pre-Reformation standard. (Our own rather infrequent village communicants certainly communicate as often as or oftener than their mediaeval forefathers.) At the same time on the Continent the Jesuits began to press for more frequent Communion. S. Ignatius in his Exercises tentatively puts it forward that ' men should

---

[1] e.g. Gregory the Great (A.D. 590–604) encourages a daily celebration at which the faithful communicate (*Dialog.* iv. 58). The Venerable Bede (A.D. 734) asks Archbishop Egbert of York to send out preachers to teach, amongst other things, how profitable is the daily reception of Christ's Body and Blood to every class of Christians.

commend the reception of the most Holy Sacrament once a year, and much more every month, and much better once a week with the requisite and due conditions.' Gradually a movement began which led to the recovery by the devout laity of the Roman obedience of weekly Communion.

In our own country since the Reformation where religion has flourished it has been marked by more frequent Communion ; where religion has declined frequent Communion has vanished with it. In Queen Anne's reign a large number of London churches had a weekly Communion with many communicants. In the eighteenth century in most places the Holy Communion was only administered once a quarter. John Wesley's preaching was often followed by a large access of communicants in the parish churches.[1] If we compare the statement that ' in that vast and noble Cathedral of S. Paul's on Easter Day, 1800, no more than six persons were found at the table of the Lord ' with what may be seen to-day even in many a village church on Sunday mornings, we shall be able to gauge the effect of the religious revival of the nineteenth century. Surely the number and frequency of Communions must be some index of the spiritual condition of our parishes.

[1] In his diary for Christmas, 1774, he writes, ' During the twelve festival days we had the Lord's Supper daily—a little emblem of the Primitive Church.'

To complete the story, in the Roman Communion the bull of Pius X, *Sacra Tridentina Synoda* (December 15, 1905), urged upon the faithful the habit of daily Communion, and it has been widely obeyed. Those who know the inner conditions of our own Church life could tell how, not at all by imitation, but by a parallel instinct, many find daily Communion to be for their soul's health, where it can be obtained. It is only natural that in broken and in restless days, when the perplexities of the individual soul are so interwoven with the confusions of society and the vast problems of world movements, that men and women should as often as they can come to Him Who gives the true Bread from heaven, and whose ordinance stands firm, though every other ground be shaking. ' Come unto Me, all ye that are weary and heavy laden, and I will refresh you.' ' They that wait upon the Lord shall renew their strength.' So it is that men and women can endure and adventure themselves on the Lord's work, still as in days of old.

Some words of S. Francis de Sales in the *Devout Life* [1] may fitly conclude our subject.

If the world asks you why you communicate so often, tell the world that it is that you may learn to love God, to purify yourself from imperfections, to deliver yourself from miseries, to find consolation in hardships and to sustain you in weakness. Tell the world that there are two kinds of people who ought to communicate often: the perfect,

[1] Part II, Chap. xxi.

because, being well disposed, it would be great wrong to keep away from the source of their perfection ; the imperfect, in order to aspire after perfection ; the strong from fear of growing weak and the weak that they may grow strong ; the healthy to be preserved from sickness and the sick to find their cure. But add for yourself, that being imperfect, weak, and sick, you need to receive often the author of perfection, the God of strength, the physician of the soul. Tell the world that those who have leisure ought to communicate often, because they have the time ; and those who are pressed with work and cares have frequent need of solid nourishment. Tell them finally that you communicate often in order to learn to communicate well, because we hardly do anything well which we practise but seldom.

THE OUTSIDER

By Joseph John Gabbett Stockley

X

THE OUTSIDER

'IS England a Christian country?' That is a question which some people will answer with an emphatic negative and others with an equally emphatic affirmative. But the question is not really an easy one to answer correctly. If by 'Christian' we mean, 'Are the majority of English people active members of the Church, or adherents of any Christian Society?' the answer is certainly 'No.' It can be conclusively proved that the great majority of the adult population of this country are outside all living and effective membership of any Christian body. If we simply mean by 'Christian' —'Are the majority baptized?' the answer is, I suppose, 'Yes.' And if we mean, 'Do the great majority still recognize some real though, it may be, rather vague authority in the life and teaching of Christ?' the answer, I would hold, is emphatically 'Yes.'

At all events, these possible answers to the great question, 'Is England a Christian country?' help us to define what we mean when we speak and write of 'the outsider.'

WHO IS THE OUTSIDER?

' The outsider ' may have been baptized,
and now be an unbeliever. Or he may have
been baptized, and have long ago ceased to take
any interest in the Christian religion. It is no
more to him than Buddhism or Hinduism.
Or—and this is very common—he may have
been baptized and may still respect Christ and
Christian things, and may have a sentimental
regard for the Church he was baptized or
married in. On the other hand ' the outsider '
may be an unbaptized person who has a warm
and genuine admiration for important parts of
the ethical teaching of our Lord.

When we talk of an ' outsider ' we do not
therefore mean that the person is an insincere
man or a bad citizen or even specially wicked.
And, knowing our own faults and failures, we
should not despise him or look down on him
in the least. Only we do hold that, on the
assumption that the Christian revelation is true,
and that it is by divine appointment enshrined
in the Church, the men and women who are
living without vital belief in this revelation and
outside the Society that witnesses for it are
living maimed, stunted, and unsatisfactory lives.
They are, we believe, like heirs of a splendid
and historic estate who refuse to possess and
enjoy what is their own. Indeed this statement of the case hardly goes far enough. For,
however true it may be that the religion of

Christ has now so extended its influence over civilized nations and social groups that people have become ashamed not to practise Christianity in some of the relations of life, it remains equally true that when heroic adventures for human welfare are desperately needed, the heroic men and women who will literally *go on risking* all in an unpopular cause are still found within and not outside the ranks of organized Christianity.

A vague admiration for Christ is indeed far better than complete indifference to His claims, but it has never been found that a vague, exalted feeling has any lasting power to strengthen the moral fibre of human beings, so as to enable them to wage a successful warfare against the attractions of a semi-paganized world without or entrenched selfishness within.

It is, then, a tragedy that ' the outsider ' remains outside the circle of Christian faith and fellowship. We cannot forget him and we ought not to ignore him. However attractive such a line of conduct may seem, it is not enough for the priests of the Church to minister to the ' remnant ' and to spend their time in striving to perfect the saints, unless they constantly bear in mind that ' the working in due measure of each several part *maketh the increase of the body* unto the building up of itself in love.'

CHRISTIANITY ESSENTIALLY PROPAGANDIST

It is nowadays almost a truism to affirm that unless Christianity is missionary and propagan-

dist it is nothing. I am sure that our good
Church people do most sincerely believe this
and that they do really desire, and, in some way
or other, work for the conversion of England
and the world to Christ. But they are appalled,
as we are all appalled, by the magnitude of the
task and the hydra-headed difficulties before us.
And yet no sincere Christian doubts that the
great work of gathering into the fold of Christ
all those who have wandered out of the way is
a solemn obligation laid upon the Church of
Christ by the Master Himself. We believe
most firmly that it is God's will that we should
' go forth into the highways and hedges ' and
compel them, by the persuasive power of divine
love, to come in. The Holy Spirit, here and
now, guides and directs our efforts, and, for
this very purpose, the strong staff of grace,
the very life of Christ Himself, is abundantly
bestowed on us in answer to our living prayers
and through the Holy Sacraments.

The work, then, is a divine work and can
only be accomplished by God. But the work
has to be done by human instruments, however
unsatisfactory. Not only is it to be remembered that, ' When Thou lettest Thy breath
go forth they shall be made and Thou shalt
renew the face of the earth,' but, the necessary
complement to the great revealing decree must
also be steadily borne in mind—' Man goeth
forth to his work and to his labour until the
evening.'

WHY IS THE OUTSIDER OUTSIDE?

So we come to the plain, human, and mundane questions : (1) Why are ' the outsiders ' living outside the Church ? and (2) What are the best means of drawing them in ?

Now if one were to ask twenty people at random why it is that so many men and women in a nominally Christian country have so little to do with the Church or any Christian body, the answers that they would give would in all probability be twenty different answers. And what is stranger still, the answers might conceivably be all true. It is easy to guess what some of their answers would be—'The Church's dogmas are outworn,' ' The Church doesn't know its own mind,' ' The bishops are too rich,' ' The clergy are so inhuman,' ' The services in church are so dull,' ' The clergy don't visit the people,' ' The services are not what they were when I was young ' (not dull enough), ' The Church has no sympathy with the working people,' ' The Church must stop trying to grovel to the Labour Party '—and so on, and so on. It is stupid to make light of these sort of answers, for they nearly all give some leading and help in a more serious inquiry.

First, I think, it ought to be frankly acknowledged that unbelief, definite or indefinite, is the primary reason why people are separated from the Church. I know that this will be denied, and the known fact of the natural piety

and religiousness of the English people will be
advanced against it. That this religiousness
is a fact no thoughtful observer of the realities
of English life can possibly deny. Except in
a very few places there is no obtrusive atheism
nor a desire to blaspheme. The anti-Christian
Sunday schools of which one reads in reactionary newspapers have not even been heard of by
the great bulk of the people in towns and villages.
More than this, one is, as a priest, greatly impressed, in visiting sick people, by the reverent
and devout behaviour of the friends and relatives who hardly ever enter a church. There
is some faith, real though indefinite. But there
is also a background of confusion, doubt, and
acquiescence in a sort of semi-conscious agnosticism. It is a condition of soul paralysis.
There is no poignant regret, no aspiration, no
initiative.

This state of mind is sometimes the result
of the person's being ignorant of what Christian teaching really is, having read one or two
clever sceptical books or magazine articles, and
having then allowed the vague generalities
which had hitherto passed for his ' faith ' to
vanish gradually from his consciousness. There
has been no real break with the past, no period
of storm and stress, no mental upheaval. Only
a gradual drifting away from anything that
could be called Christian membership, and an
imperceptible change of view. Now that the
conventional adherence to the outward forms

of religion—such as church-going on Sunday mornings—has ceased to be demanded by fashion and respectability, the practices of religion are given up, and with them, inevitably, religion itself. Above all, the man ceases to pray, even privately.

Or the influence of the daily press—often the only sort of reading he indulges in—gradually operates on the mind of the average church-goer. The English press is not deliberately anti-Christian, but, in the daily newspapers, religion is habitually treated as a matter of very minor interest. It comes long after sport, finance, politics. Only when controversies become so acute that personalities are engaged in, or when a toothsome scandal about some unhappy clergyman is brought to public notice, do the headlines loom large.

It is not fair to blame the daily press for this. Newspapers are written to satisfy the demands of the public, and the editors know their business. But the effects on the ordinary reader of this sort of presentation of religious ' news ' is real, and often permanent. Gradually the idea—that it is right for a sensible man to ' seek *first* the kingdom of God and His righteousness '—passes away completely from the mind. Christ has been dethroned from the supreme position, and has become either a pious memory, or an impossibly unpractical dreamer, or (as a Continental writer once put it) merely the head of the clerical interest.

It would of course be unfair to ignore altogether the case of those who, having been Christians of a definite type, have after careful consideration given up Christianity because unable any longer to believe in the supernatural claims of Christ. There are many such people now, as heretofore, but their numbers are, in proportion to the masses of the non-church-going population, very small. They form indeed a grave and a pressing problem, but a problem the Church has always had to reckon with in every country and in every age. What is peculiar to England of to-day is the wide and strong drift away from Church membership of those who are not of this type at all.

The many excellent and thoroughly up-to-date books being written in defence of the Faith show that earnestly genuine efforts are being made to combat unbelief. The real unbelievers are being catered for. It is the multitude of men and women who are no convinced unbelievers and who could not understand these books if they troubled to read them—they are the crux of the problem.

How is he to be Brought Back?

How are we to get them back? Or at all events stop the drifting away from the Church? First of all, by a radical alteration of the methods adopted in religious teaching of the young.

Notwithstanding all that has been said or

written, it is still, I am convinced, true that in most schools, whether elementary, secondary, or public, 'religious teaching' still means teaching children and adolescents about religion. Sometimes the teaching is fairly definite and is carefully given, and sometimes it is unintelligent and misty. But how seldom is the objective, the aim, right. It cannot be too frequently and earnestly pressed that the object of religious teaching is not merely to instruct the mind in the truths of the Faith but to train the child or person to love and serve God and therefore to become religious.

There is among us even now the notion that religion and the practices of religion have nothing much to do with each other. So we have everywhere many young people who can pass examinations in religious knowledge, but who (not through their own fault) know little of what prayer, repentance, worship, mean, and who cannot be said to have any true sense of the claims of Jesus Christ upon their lives. If this be not the case, how does it happen that while 'religious teaching' in our great Public Schools is given daily, the number of vocations to the sacred ministry from these schools is so small as to be almost negligible ? It is really useless —and it may be worse than useless—to persist in teaching religion as if it were simply a 'subject' to be taught among many other subjects. Religion is an atmosphere to be breathed and a life to be lived. It is, as again and again has been said, 'caught' as well as taught, and it can only be passed on through personalities to personalities. 'The child's mind is not a vase to be filled but a fire to be kindled.'

It will naturally be objected that to demand an alteration in the fundamental methods of training the young people in religion will not call back or bring into the Church those who are outside. But it is surely true wisdom to look forward, and so to train our boys and girls who are now within the fold, that the great army of backsliders may not be ceaselessly reinforced from the ranks of those who were once ' fellow citizens with the saints and of the household of God.'

Secondly, we are bound to believe (and I *ex animo* do believe) that the lapsed can in large numbers be recovered and many of ' the outsiders ' converted to Christ if the clergy and other Church workers really manifest the love of God in their lives and ministrations. Of course the clergy are absurdly few in numbers for the vast work. It is almost impossible to estimate our feebleness in this respect, and never did Christ's words seem more intensely applicable than in the England of to-day. 'But when He saw the multitudes, He was moved with compassion for them, because they were distressed and scattered, as sheep not having a shepherd. Then saith He unto His disciples, The harvest truly is plenteous, but the labourers are few. Pray ye therefore the Lord of the harvest, that He send forth labourers into His harvest.'

We are few indeed, but the first few Apostles did wonders, and the first few Franciscans, and the first few Methodists, and the first few Oxford leaders of 1834.

Religion is ever an incalculable force, and if only men have faith and if the fire of the Spirit is within them, great and unexpected happenings will occur. After all, isn't it true that pastoral and evangelistic work carried out by men who have the temper and outlook of a Stanton, a Dolling, a Watts-Ditchfield, has always succeeded ? And, while we assuredly do need to know the Faith in its essence and in its present-day implications, and while we realize that we must be trained to teach it simply and systematically, we are acutely conscious that the pressing and crying need of the time is for men who can make a ' popular ' appeal in the true and legitimate sense of that much abused word. Such men must, above all, show that they naturally care for the people to whom they minister. Father Dolling had one supreme test of the effectiveness of a parish priest. He would say to his friends in parishes: ' Do you love your people ? '

In his admirable Preface to Professor Brilioth's learned work on *The Anglican Revival* the Bishop of Gloucester writes :

In what did the weakness of the Oxford Movement lie ? Of course in its early days there was much crude thought and many crude ideas. New realms of religion, life, and thought were being discovered and explored, and often the knowledge was imperfect and the deductions inadequate. That will always be the case. I do not think that it is here the weakness of the movement lies. I think it lies and always has lain in its failure in its popular appeal. It has always been academic, appealing rather to the cultivated than to the great body of the people ; and at the present day it has very little hold on the great mass of the English people. They have learnt some things from it. It has changed and stimulated the life of the Anglican community. It has enabled it to adapt itself to its new conditions as a cosmopolitan representative of Christianity ; but it has never been able to take hold of the mass of the people as Wesleyanism or Evangelicalism did in their time, and the English Church will not be able to fulfil its task unless it adds the religion of emotion and experience to the religion of institutions and the intellectual life.

Of course the Anglo-Catholics are only a section of the English Church. But they are an important section and are not likely to become less important. If Anglo-Catholicism can produce priests who can live and teach ' the religion of emotion and experience,' then the Church will most assuredly gather in a large number of those who are now ' out of the way.' In preaching, visiting, holding missions, what are now wanted immediately are many priests and lay-workers (whether members of Religious Orders or not) who truly believe that the love of Christ constrains them, and who are saturated through and through with the triumphant ideas S. Paul set forth in 1 Corinthians xiii : ' Love never faileth.'

It is fatally easy to criticize, but is there not some truth in the view taken by the average man that orthodoxy of belief often seems to produce hardness, arrogance, a repellent manner, and a closed mind ?   If, on the other hand, an Englishman sees and knows religious people who are attractive because of their religion he is impressed, and he may become willing to listen to a presentation of the truth that is new to him.   But—unlike the Scot—he is not naturally a theologian, neither is he a mystic.   He is, as a matter of fact, a pragmatist through and through, and, while he has largely lost faith in institutional religion, he will follow a live personality who seems to him to have some ' family likeness ' to Christ.

Especially must this sort of appeal be made in preaching.   It is striking to notice the real and persistent success of preachers who with no special intellectual power are nevertheless able to impress their hearers with the living truth of the compassionateness of God.   They are able to become Christ's instruments for binding up the broken-hearted and proclaiming liberty to sin's captives.   These are the men to gather in the outsiders.

It should be the same in our visiting.   The lamentable shortage of clergy in our large towns —and, by the way, the monstrous growth of time-wasting organizations and conferences— make visiting on an extended scale increasingly difficult.   Yet it remains true that we cannot influence our people unless we know them. And there is no possible chance of drawing in the outsiders to the fold of Christ unless, by any and every means in our power, we strive to get into touch with them.

I do not profess to have had first-hand knowledge of the 'Crusades' organized by the Industrial Christian Fellowship, but competent witnesses assure me that remarkable results have already been achieved through these special efforts. What needs emphasizing is that, whether in visiting, or in Crusades, or in ordinary personal intercourse with our people, those who represent the Church shall remember every moment that they are trustees not only for the Faith Christ taught but also for the love wherewith—in spite of desperate discouragement—He loved sinful, and often stupid, men and women unto the end. If we are to succeed in the great enterprise we have at all costs to change radically the average view that the outsider takes of 'religious people.' Men like Stanton and Dolling were, I suppose—like poets—'born not made.' But we hold that divine grace can work miracles, and that if our temperaments are not 'naturally Christian' we can become Christian if we believe the transformation is possible. 'Love never faileth.'

THE OBSTACLE OF PARTY STRIFE

This is far from being a controversial essay, but it is necessary to say that if we want to draw

the outsiders into Christian fellowship, this
Christian fellowship must be a reality, and party
strife in the Church of England must cease.
However difficult it is to define what is essential
and what is not, there must at least be a stead-
fast determination to strive after the ideal
expressed in the words—' In things essential,
unity : in things indifferent, variety : in all
things, charity.' Personally, I believe we are
well on the way to attain this ideal and manifest
it to the world. On all hands there is a growing
desire to learn from those with whom we do
not agree, and a growing recognition of the
good work done by men who would, a few years
ago, have been looked on as adversaries.

Of course there goes with all this the great
danger of indifference to religious truth. It is
far from easy to decide where tolerance ends
and facile acquiescence in falsehood begins.
But to those whose belief in the Holy Ghost
carries with it a practical faith that He is *now*
guiding the Church and each member of it,
the fact that a line of action may be dangerous
will not hinder its being adopted. If we believe
—as we do believe—that, in a world of fresh
and vast opportunities, and full of disillusioned
nations, classes, and individuals, God's call to
go forth and witness for Him is insistent, then
we must forget a great deal, and risk a great
deal, if we are to ' lift Christ up ' in such a way
that ' all men may be drawn unto Him.' As
Anglicans we have been inclined to stress over-

much the virtues of tact and caution. Zeal
and even recklessness are what we need now.

Conclusion

Finally, I plead that by every means possible
we remind our communicants that the Church
is not in possession of England but is on a
mission to England. While we minister to
the hundreds within, let us not for a moment
forget the thousands outside the fold. Let
this most pressing of questions be constantly
brought before our Parochial Church Councils
and our great organizations for men and
women, such as the Church of England Men's
Society and the Mothers' Union.

I know well that the ' Establishment '—and all
that dreary word connotes—is a heavy obstacle
in our path. Let us ignore it and go on teaching that religion is dynamic and not static. The
younger people will gladly respond, and they
are the future Church. The question is, can
we make them become missionaries, propagan-
dists ? If true faith is ours ; if our activities
are permeated by prayer ; if, above all, the
Holy Sacraments are centres from which the
divine life is drawn for sacrifice and service,
and not simply for personal satisfaction, then
we are bound to look forward to the certain
fulfilment of the promises of God. He will
draw home to Himself ' those that are turned
back from following the Lord.'

FOREIGN MISSIONS

By the Bishop in Corea

XI

FOREIGN MISSIONS

OUR Lord's plan for the redemption of the world plainly involves the Church which He founded in a twofold responsibility. She has, in reliance on the Holy Spirit bequeathed by Him and by the faithful use of 'the Doctrine and Sacraments and the Discipline,' committed to her charge—

(*a*) To work unceasingly for the extension of that kingdom, of which He laid the foundations, until it includes the whole human race within its borders and all the peoples of the world become 'one flock under one shepherd.'

(*b*) To feed, shepherd, sustain, and govern those who have been already admitted within the fold and enrolled as citizens of the kingdom, in order that they may walk worthily of the vocation wherewith they are called and live up to the privileges and responsibilities which their citizenship involves.

The misfortune is that, with the latter duty lying so close to their hands and making such obvious and immediate demands on their energies, members of the Church (clergy and laity alike) are only too apt to lose their sense of

proportion, and, if they do not overlook altogether the Church's duty of constantly expand-
ing her borders, at least relegate it to a position
of very secondary importance as compared with
the duty of ministering to those already within
the fold.   Surely it ought hardly to need stating
that it is no more possible to compound for the
neglect of the one by the attempted fulfilment
of the other duty in this respect, than it is in the
parallel case of one's duty towards God and
one's duty towards one's neighbour.

For us in the Church of England the issue
has been much confused by the extensive
emigration of our own kith and kin to the
' regions beyond '—most often to the vast un-
peopled spaces of the earth in the American
and Australasian continents.   And the task of
ministering to these emigrated brethren of ours
has been unfortunately too long confounded—
under the misleadingly comprehensive title of
' overseas work '—with the totally different
task of propagating the Faith among the still
countless non-Christian races of the globe.[1] But
surely it ought to be clearly understood, as a
general principle, that the duty of caring for
our brethren in the great overseas dominions of
the British Empire is really only an extension

---

[1] In some cases, notably in South Africa, the bishops have
the double burden to bear, though even here the conditions
and requirements of the two sides of the work are so diverse
that it appears to be difficult to avoid keeping them more or
less in separate water-tight compartments.

of the ordinary parochial and pastoral work of
the Church, and a duty of which the home
Church ought to be relieved as soon as the
various colonial Churches, many of which are a
hundred years old and more, have been fairly
set upon their feet. In any case the problems
of the two kinds of ' overseas work ' are so
dissimilar that it is impossible to treat of them
together in such a chapter as this. What
follows is written in view of the requirements,
and by one who has (apart from parochial
work in England) only experience, of what
may be strictly described as ' missions to the
heathen.'

Preliminary Notes

This of course is not the place to preach a
homily to the clergy on 'the importance of
missions.' But as a background for what is
to follow, it may not be amiss briefly to lay
stress on two points.

1. Note first the extraordinary smallness of
the area as yet won for Christ and covered by
what we may describe as organized Christendom. Close on twenty centuries have passed
since our Lord launched the Catholic Church
on its world-wide mission, and still, even if we
bring every species of Christianity—Catholic
and Protestant, orthodox, heretical, and schis-
matic—into the reckoning, a full two-thirds
of the world's population are left, through the
sloth and selfishness of generations of Chris-

tians, outside the range of the covenanted mercies of God.

Having allowed herself to be hemmed in by Islam to the East and the South, as she was already shut in by the Arctic and Atlantic Oceans to the North and the West, the Christian Church, for all her charter of Catholicity, seems quite deliberately for the best part of a thousand years, with some rare and noble exceptions,[1] to have limited her vision to the races living within that relatively tiny *enclave* of the world's surface which is practically conterminous with the modern continent of Europe, and to have settled down more or less contentedly to the task of elaborating her doctrine and ceremonial for their behoof. And this habit of mind has become so ingrained—and that not least among Catholics—as to be by no means dead even yet. In this way many precious centuries were lost, and, during those centuries, possibly as a punishment for her selfish narrowness of vision, the Church's pristine unity was shattered. Thus when, in the early days of the nineteenth century, Christians awoke

[1] Such as the great ' Nestorian ' Missions in Central and Eastern Asia ; the efforts of S. Francis and S. Raymond Lull to penetrate the Mahometan world ; the great Franciscan Missions of the thirteenth and fourteenth centuries to China (which, alas ! perished without leaving any mark behind) ; and the wonderful efforts put forth in the sixteenth, seventeenth, and eighteenth centuries in Eastern Asia, South America, and elsewhere by the Jesuits and other missionary organizations of the Roman Catholic Church.

once more to the world-wide character of the
task committed by Christ to His Church, it was
a disordered and disunited Christendom which
had to face the fact that practically all the great
continent of Asia with its vast populations
and wonderful old civilizations, all the black
continent of Africa with its myriads of child-
races, and all ' the islands of the sea ' were still
'sitting in darkness and the shadow of death.'

Vast efforts have been made, in spite of our
unhappy divisions, by Protestant and Catholic
alike, within the last hundred years or so to
make up for lost time. And in these the
Church of England has taken a considerable,
though by no means a leading, part. But even
so it still remains true that probably far less
than one per cent. of the immense populations
of the Far East (China, Japan, Corea, Siam,
etc.) has as yet been won to Christianity of any
kind, while in Africa the situation has developed
into a ' neck and neck ' struggle between Christianity and Islam, and even in a country subject
for so long to Christian influences as India,
Christians of every colour and kind do not
number more than five millions out of the
total population of three hundred and twenty
millions.

2. In the second place it is worth noting
how haphazard and ill-proportioned have been
such missionary efforts as the Church of
England has made. Whatever faults one may
feel inclined to find with the presentation of

the missionary case in the recently published
' World Call,' one may be thankful that at last
an attempt has been made to envisage the *whole*
task that still lies ahead of the Church—and to
envisage it *as a whole*. But this has not been
so in the past. And least of all has it been so
with those to whom the name of ' Catholic '
is most dear. Arresting figures like Bishop
Patteson or the Selwyns, Bishop Steere and
the long and noble line of his successors in
Central Africa, crying scandals like the African
slave trade, political developments like the
gradual spread of the British Empire over a
large part of the globe, have all indeed helped
to stir the sluggish conscience of the Church
at home. But very little attempt has hitherto
been made to correlate the tasks thus brought
to the Church's notice, to draw her attention
to those vast fields, like China and the Far East,
which have lacked such advertisement, or to
estimate the relative importance of the fields
thus laid open to her vision and to dispose of
her available forces accordingly.

Thus it is remarkable that, while the Catholic
wing of the English Church has given lavishly
and of its best to Africa, Asia has been to a
large extent left without such succour, with
results which are already beginning to react
painfully on the Church at home and will be
found to react more painfully still, if the
balance is not redressed. And yet Asia is
the great mother of us all—mother of races,

mother of tongues, mother of religions—enclosing within her capacious bosom more than one half of the world's inhabitants, most of them civilized with a civilization far older and in many ways, saving only Christianity, more remarkable than our own. No missionary programme which leaves Asia out, or fails to give Asia the foremost place it deserves, can claim to be loyal to our Lord's commission to ' make disciples of all nations.'

Here again the issue is often confused by such a purely political happening as the widespread of the British Empire. And there are not lacking those who tell us that the Church of England ought rigidly to confine herself to those races which have come under British sway. It is a little difficult to see how any such contention can find support for itself in the pages of the New Testament or in the practice of the Church Catholic. It is indeed but one form of Erastus' monstrous *dictum*—'*cujus regio, ejus religio*.' And when one realizes the terrible complications which have arisen (e.g. in India both in ancient and modern times) from the concentration of the forces of political power and Christian evangelization in the hands of one and the same race, one is sometimes tempted to wonder whether it would not be preferable to entrust the propagation of the Faith in any given country to any people rather than those who hold political power therein !

The Starting-point—God's Call

For the individual priest, of course, the question whether he should devote himself to the mission field, and, if so, to what part of the mission field he should go, must remain in the last resort a matter of ' vocation.' For just as the priesthood itself is a matter of ' vocation,' so we have to remember that within the priesthood of the Catholic Church there are ' diversities of operations,' which themselves depend on the calling of God. As a priest has to decide for himself, under the guidance of the Holy Spirit, whether he is called to the pastoral life of a parish priest in the home (or colonial) Church, to an academic and literary ministry in school or college, to the life of a ' religious ' or a ' secular ' priest, or even, in the providence of God, to rise from the ranks of the presbyterate to the episcopate, so every priest must at some time in his career fairly face the question whether God does not mean him to devote himself to a missionary apostolate in heathen lands, outside the charmed circle of organized Christendom.

Of course in such a matter there are many issues to be taken into consideration, and in order to give them all due weight it is well to fortify one's wavering determination by having recourse to those whose advice one knows to be worth taking. Still it remains true that, in such a crisis, a man's heart will often tell him more that is worth his knowing than

' seven men in a high tower.' And there are not lacking those who have lived to bless the day when, in the assurance of a clear call, they shook themselves free, at whatever temporary cost on both sides, from the force of family ties, the insistent advice of worldly friends or —more difficult still—the well-meant counsel of that gentle tyrant of to-day—the doctor.

Nor in view of the many difficulties, linguistic and other, lying ahead of the missionary to the heathen, is it possible to be patient with palliatives and half measures such as are recommended to us under the expression ' short service.' Short of a clear call to return such as took one away from home, surely the term of one's natural life is the proper period of service abroad.

On any showing, this question of vocation is of course of crucial importance—both for the priest who goes and for him who concludes to stay at home. Both at some time in their career will inevitably pass through dark periods when they will be tempted to regard their ministry as a failure. And both will find in such dark moments unspeakable comfort in the recollection that they did honestly wrestle with the question of ' vocation,' before choosing the line of their life's work. When wavering faith seems likely enough to allow us to be swallowed up whole, we shall speedily find ourselves upheld by the outstretched hand of Him Who bade us ' Come,' and Who will chide us now, as He chid Peter of old, with the word of loving rebuke, 'Wherefore didst thou doubt?'

The Missionary's Goal

So we begin at the beginning—with the call of God. And what is to be the end? 'Whatsoever thou takest in hand,' said the Wise Man, 'remember the end and thou shalt never do amiss.' What then is to be the end, the goal, the aim, which the missionary priest in non-Christian lands is to set before him? In the good old Evangelical days the salvation of the 'perishing heathen' by individual conversion seemed good enough as a goal. But nowadays we do not feel quite so able as our forefathers to share the cheery pessimism of a S. Francis Xavier, who when asked as to the fate of the ancestors of his noble Japanese converts, is said to have replied : ' *Omnes damnati.*'

As one lives among many of these non-Christian folk and studies their history and realizes how many noble and lovable characters their old-world culture or religion has produced, one cannot but find oneself indefinitely extending the range of the uncovenanted mercies of God and indulging in the larger hope for those whom lack of opportunity or invincible ignorance have kept outside the city of God. Moreover, it is surely a very poor appreciation of the Gospel of the Incarnation which represents it as an offering to one here and another there—as brands snatched from the burning—a merely individual and negative gift. Rather do we go forth charged with the task of communicating to ' the nations ' the great positive gift of the Grace and Truth which came by Jesus Christ, and of offering to them the inestimable blessing of enrolment as citizens of the great city of God, with all the privileges in this world and the next which that citizenship carries with it.

Thus, though we missionaries inevitably begin as pioneers with the conversion of individuals in this country or in that, we have to keep ever before ourselves, as our ultimate aim, the setting up therein of the city of God— a very member of the One, Holy, Catholic, Apostolic Church—fully organized and fully equipped with Creeds, Sacraments, Ministry, and Liturgy, and all else that is necessary to enable our children in the Faith to live the Christ-life themselves, and to bring their brethren and sisters to the fold. Then, as parish after parish, diocese after diocese, is set upon its feet, we ' foreign ' priests must be content to leave the work thus built up by ourselves to our brethren of the ' native ' ministry, giving them what incidental help and supervision they need, while we pass on to break up fallow ground elsewhere.

Importance of Native Ministry

It is the more necessary to insist upon this just because we English clergy are all too ready to carry our parochialism with us and to become so wedded to ' my work,' ' my Church,' ' my parish,' as to leave the ' native ' Church and ministry no chance for self-development, no opportunity of learning by experience to bear their own burdens. Not only, however, is it unfair to the infant Church thus to subject it to interminable spoon-feeding, but a moment's consideration will suffice to show that, if the home Church is not only to provide missionaries to ' propagate ' the Faith, but also for an indefinite period to find pastors to shepherd the newly formed flocks, an *impasse* will soon be reached ; as no possible increase in the supply of ordination candidates at home will ever suffice to fill all the available posts.

Thus, as soon as ever his individual conversions have provided him with a field large enough to choose from, the missionary priest must set himself to work to develop among his younger neophytes the sense of vocation to the ministry, and the missionary bishop to provide the opportunities of theological and devotional training which will enable these vocations to find their fulfilment. No other work can compare in importance with this, if the Church is ever to take real and effectual root. The ' native ' Christian ought never to be allowed to regard the ' foreign ' priest or bishop as more than a temporary and provisional part of the furniture of his Church.

Side by side with this development of the

native ministry must inevitably go the inculca-
tion of the duty of financial self-support. For
the missionary priest himself, the line of least
resistance is to go on depending as long as
possible on remittances from the society or
association in the home-land. And the 'native'
Christian, being but human, is more than
willing to have it so. But an Indian, African,
Chinese, Japanese, or Corean Church, whose
' native' clergy remain indefinitely on the pay-
roll of a society in Europe, or which depends
helplessly on remittances from a 'foreign'
country for its working expenses, is plainly in
a very unhealthy condition. Gifts to cover
capital expenditure, as for the erection of
churches, or for the supply of ornaments, vestments, etc., obviously do not lie open to the
same objection—especially as, for lack of any
tradition on the subject, the plan or design for
such things must in early days be supplied
from a 'foreign' source. But even here the
spirit of self help should be developed as soon
as possible, and every opportunity of self-
expression should be given to the 'native'
artist, once he is saturated with the Catholic
atmosphere.

Educational and Medical Institutions

In this connection a word should perhaps be
said as to the part which schools, hospitals, and
similar institutions may play in the pioneer
stage of the Church's work in non-Christian

lands. And here it is important to realize how completely the circumstances of the mission field have changed within the last thirty years. Until the end of the nineteenth century medical science had made such little headway outside the European and American continents, and there were large regions of the earth's surface where anything in the shape of education, in the modern sense, was so unknown that offers on the part of a missionary body to open a school or hospital were readily accepted almost everywhere. And such mission schools and hospitals have in the past undoubtedly played an invaluable part in the *praeparatio evangelica*.

Almost inevitably, however, those in charge of such institutions have in many cases slipped by degrees into the position of claiming for themselves a general leadership in such matters with a doubly unfortunate result. For in the first place such leadership can only be maintained nowadays by a growing elaboration of plant and increase of expenditure, with which no conceivable ' native ' Church would ever be in a position to saddle itself. And in the second place, it has to be remembered that nowadays it is hard to find any corner of the globe which is not either under the tutelage of some nominally Christian and civilized Western power, or else the realm of some intensely race-conscious government, like those of Turkey, China, Japan, Siam, and the like, which are increasingly well supplied with educational and medical organizations of their own. And in both cases (with some rare exceptions, chiefly in the British Empire) it is not too much to say that such governments are increasingly unwilling to hand over their educational and medical responsibilities to foreign bodies, however charitable, or to allow schools and hospitals to be used for the purpose of any propaganda other than that of national and patriotic sentiment.

The present writer's experience would lead him to say that, in any country where religious propaganda is allowed at all, no objection is likely to be made to schools or hospitals which are content to play a modest rôle, ancillary to the general life of the infant Church, but that any attempt to enter into competition with government institutions, or to dominate the educational or medical situation (besides its financial hopelessness, unless you have a Rockefeller behind you), will meet with increasingly stern and stubborn resistance from the ' powers that be.'

The missionary priest of the future will therefore in all probability find himself less and less under any temptation to be side-tracked into grandiose schemes of this kind, and will have the advantage of being the more able to concentrate his energies on the spiritual side of his work. And throughout it all he must be for ever conscious and for ever pressing it

s

on the consciousness of his flock that the Church
which he is engaged in building up is theirs
and not his. Like our Lord's precursor he
must be willing to 'decrease,' while they
'increase,' and—while willing to spend himself
to his uttermost breath on their behalf—to welcome every step which brings both him and
them nearer the day when his children in the
Faith shall be able safely to dispense with his
leading strings and to 'stand upon their feet,'
free with the freedom of children in the house
of our common Father, the 'large room'
of God's One, Holy, Catholic, Apostolic
Church.

Practical Considerations on Life and Work

We have spoken of the *beginning*—that sense
of 'vocation' which must lie at the root of all
true work for God. We have envisaged the
end—that setting up of the city of God, which
must be the aim of all legitimate missionary
endeavour. What of the *means*, whereby we
may proceed from the beginning to the end,
fulfilling our vocation and compassing our
aim ?

(*a*) First and foremost, it goes without saying
that, in the mission field almost more than
anywhere else, it matters more what a man is
than what he does. The missionary priest
must be recognized by those among whom he
lives, Christian and pagan alike, as a 'man of

God,' as one who is in intimate touch with the Unseen. And only those who have lived in the spiritually depressing atmosphere of a starkly pagan land will know how difficult it is to maintain with steadiness a high standard of spiritual life and personal devotion. Our missionary will need, here more than elsewhere, all the familiar helps to be found in the regular recitation of his offices, the frequent offering of the Holy Sacrifice, the use of the Sacrament of Penance, the yearly Retreat, and—almost more than all—the daily exercise of mental prayer or meditation, without which (and the present writer speaks with a humiliating consciousness of his own failure) any or all of the rest are apt to become hard, dry, mechanical. In the unceasing round of visits to outlying stations, not seldom at a distance from his centre, and frequently a victim to trying climatic conditions, the missionary priest will often find himself almost hopelessly impeded in his daily private devotions. The only possible course is to determine and adhere to as manageable a rule of life as possible for these periods of discomfort and unrest, and to make the most of the times of comparative quiet which intervene, never for one moment losing sight of the ideal.

(*b*) In outward demeanour our missionary must 'abstain from all appearance of evil' and 'let his moderation be known unto all men.' Low as the standard of conduct among his

non-Christian neighbours may be, they will be
the first to note and criticize severely any depar-
ture from the high (and possibly exaggerated)
standard of conduct they demand from a leader
of the Christians. And the Christians themselves will be mortified and discouraged by any
lapse—I do not say, God forbid, into open
sin, but—into frivolous or unseemly behaviour,
which lays their pastor open to the criticisms
of their non-Christian neighbours. The rough
and ready comradeship, the ' hail-fellow-well-
met ' *bonhomie*, which may not be out of place
in an English mining village or an East End
Boys' Club, will not of necessity be found to
be much of a recommendation to the good
opinion of the average Asiatic, or even the un-
tutored African. And quite as important as a
grave and discreet manner—which the constant
wearing of the ecclesiastical habit will go far
to secure—is the avoidance of anything like
hastiness, brusquerie, and ill temper, whatever
the provocation, in dealing with Christian and
heathen alike. The simple Christian finds it
hard to understand—and harder still to defend
—such a plain infraction of Gospel principles
as appears to him to be involved in a sudden
ebullition of unrestrained anger ; while patience and a simple kindly civility will carry one
far in all circles.

(*c*) It is of course impossible to give any
general rules as to the best method of getting
into touch with and influencing those whom it

is the missionary's office to bring to the Faith.
'The Lord knoweth them that are His,' and
'The Spirit bloweth where it listeth.' And
though in every mission field one must be
content to bear patiently with periods of
arrested opportunity, there is no limit to the
varied and often surprising ways in which points
of contact will be found—most often, when
once a start has been made, through the good
offices of a ' native worker ' (the best missionaries to their own people) or some simple
soul, who has already found his way into the
fold.

But, without any possibility of contradiction,
it is the missionary priest's duty to identify
himself as far as possible with the people of his
adopted country. He will certainly be of no
use, in most mission fields, unless he is prepared
to submit to the tiresome drudgery of learning
their language and the irksomeness of adapting himself to their harmless social customs ;
though he will certainly also be well advised to
avoid making himself ridiculous by any *outré*
aping of 'native' manners or endeavouring to
conceal the fact, patent enough to every one,
that he is a ' foreigner.' On the other hand,
nothing can well be more offensive or more fatal
to his influence—especially in these days of
exaggerated race-consciousness—than any assumption of social or racial superiority, based
on the mere fact of his Western birth and
education. And if he really ' loves his people '

—Father Dolling's golden rule for all mission priests—it will be difficult for him to avoid interesting himself in the history and literature, the scenery and natural history, the folk-lore, the arts, and the domestic economy of his adopted fellow-countrymen, and above all in those ancient religions which have hitherto stood to them in the place of the Gospel. For all of these will in their measure help him to understand the real workings of the ' native ' mind, however much these may be hidden, especially among the rising generation, by an affected contempt for their own old culture and a hollow pose of admiring and mimicking only the ill-understood and ill-digested culture of the West.

At all costs he will avoid entangling himself in the secular and political affairs of the community in which he lives, recognizing his hopeless incapacity as a ' foreigner ' to find his way through such a maze, and recognizing also that, as the world is constituted now, he is everywhere the guest of some responsible government, who suffer his presence there and have a right to demand that he shall not harass them by meddling with affairs outside his *métier*. It is true that even under a ' civilized ' government of the twentieth century the missionary priest may find himself in a position where religious principle may make it necessary for him to stand in opposition to the powers that be—and take the consequences. But he will do well to

reckon beforehand with the fact that those consequences nowadays are not likely to take the
shape of anything heroic in the form of the
torture-chamber, the stake, or the block, but
for his flock a petty and underhand police
persecution, and for himself, in the last resort,
deportation and permanent exclusion from the
country.

(*d*) In dealing with his inquirers and catechumens, and even his neophyte Christians,
let the missionary priest be very tender and
patient—patient even with their mixed motives
in coming to him and their slowness to appreciate the real drift of the Gospel which he brings
them. He may well remind himself from time
to time how even those who were brought into
direct contact with our Lord could plague Him
with querulous requests like S. Peter's ' What
shall we have therefore ? ' or with impossible
demands for the right and the left hand thrones
in His kingdom, and he should remember
too how any religious practices of which his
converts have had experience in their pre-
Christian days have almost invariably had
material benefit in view.

Patience and wisdom will also be needed in
resolutely putting first things first and laying
firmly and well ' the foundations of repentance
from dead works and of faith towards God '
and the other ' principles of the doctrine of
Christ,' before going on to emphasize details
of ceremonial observance or devotional practice,

which happen to have been forced into a
position of temporary prominence by the
exigencies of Church polemics in the home-
land. It is probably not unfair to say that
questions of liturgical observance and details of
devotional practice have almost inevitably occupied so much attention during the last seventy
years of the Catholic revival in England, that
an English missionary priest is in greater risk
than another of losing his sense of the ' proportion of faith.' And in so doing he may forget
that his fundamental task consists in the introduction of his neophytes, not to a mere round of
liturgical observances, but to an entirely new
' way ' of life, an entirely new attitude to the
God Who made him and the world in which he
lives, of which liturgical and devotional practices
are the efflorescence, as necessary indeed to his
spiritual life, as foliage and flowers to the health
of the tree, and yet not to be emphasized
at the expense of the root, the stem, or the
fruit.

If we may assume a generally Catholic
outlook at the start, any properly organized
diocese in the mission field will have the opportunity of settling for itself in Synod vexed
questions of ceremonial detail or devotional
practice, without tying itself to the chariot
wheels of ' movements ' or organizations in
the Church at home which have not the same
problems to envisage. For this reason, among
others, it is of great importance that a mis-

sionary bishop should as early as possible in the history of his diocese begin summoning his Diocesan Synod and letting that be the instrument through which he governs the flock committed to his charge. For after all it must be remembered that the diocese, and not the province or patriarchate, still less the individual priest, is the fundamental unit of Church life.

(*e*) Next let an earnest plea be made for an unbounded sympathy with the 'native' priests and assistant workers, and for a great tenderness for the failings of the ordinary 'native' Christian. If one is tempted to lose heart at the grievous lapse from time to time of one of these last, let us remind ourselves that it is very difficult for us to realize the force of the temptations to which they are exposed. Let us bethink ourselves also of the sort of conduct against which S. Paul found it necessary to be constantly warning his neophyte converts at Corinth, Colosse, or Ephesus, and remember that our converts, like his, have centuries of bad tradition and heredity to live down through the power of the Holy Spirit and the grace of our Lord Jesus Christ imparted through the Sacraments. We hold, thank God, the key of the position in the Sacrament of Penance. And one can never be thankful enough for the clearness with which our Christians recognize this and for the all-but certainty, won by experience, that sooner or later the straying

sheep will by this means find his way back to
the fold.

And, as for our ' native ' priests and other
workers, how greatly they need all the help,
encouragement, and sympathy we can give
them in carrying out the task, which we without
their aid should be helpless to compass ! With
all the aids we English priests get from books
and magazines, from wise advisers, from the
companionship of fellow priests, from retreats
and conferences, from tradition and environ-
ment, and from the pressure of a public opinion
which is at least fundamentally Christian, how
difficult we find it to be what we ought or to do
what we should ! And for them, who have
hardly any of these helps, what a miracle it is,
what a testimony to the grace of Holy Orders,
that they should do as well as they do, what a
challenge they make to us to offer them all the
help that lies in our power ! For himself the
present writer cannot speak warmly enough of
the standard maintained, the example set, and
the work done — often under very difficult
conditions—by those ' native ' clergy whom it
has been his privilege to raise to the priesthood.

(*f*) Something of course ought to have been
said about the special difficulties of dealing with
women and children. But considerations of
space make it impossible to do more than to
lay emphasis on one fact about each. First,
with regard to the women, it is impossible to

overestimate the force of the upheaval which has recently befallen the life of a large part of the non-Christian world in the absolute *bouleversement* of all the old ideas of the relations between the sexes. This upheaval has, of course, its sources in the West, but has led to a situation in the East compared with which the parallel revolution in the West is but child's play. The Church's answer to this must be to create a ministry of ' native ' women to their sisters. And for this purpose we cannot begin too soon holding up the possibility of vocation to the 'religious life' before the eyes of our neophyte maidens. Of the children, let it be said at once that the practice of infant Baptism brings with it in the mission field difficulties at least as great as those which beset the parish priest at home, while it is difficult to make the sponsorial responsibility much more real in the one case than the other. Christians often live at great distances from one another and from the nearest church, so that there must inevitably be large numbers of christened children who fall outside the range of any Sunday School or Catechism net which the missionary may spread. All the more, therefore, it behoves the mission priest on his rounds to have in mind the infant as well as the adult members of his flock, and to see to it that no pains are spared to secure for them an adequate training in the Faith into which they have been baptized, if he would not saddle the infant Church with the scandal of multitudes of 'baptized heathen,' with which in home lands we are only too familiar.

'OUR UNHAPPY DIVISIONS' IN THE MISSION FIELD

If nothing has been said above about difficulties arising from the presence of other missionaries in the field, it is because the present writer is convinced that the difficulties arising from this (though they do of course exist) have been quite unnecessarily exaggerated, and that, most often, by those who have an axe to grind on the subject of a one-sided reunion with the Protestant bodies. The field is so vast that in countries composed, as most Asiatic and African countries are in the main, of small village communities, there is no reason why, with the exercise of ordinary prudence and charity, there need be any serious overlapping for centuries to come. And by that time we may hope that the reunion of Christendom will have passed beyond the stage of 'conversations' at Malines or elsewhere.

In the meanwhile let us never forget that, inasmuch as the future Church in any given country will certainly not be an exact replica of our own mission or of any of the other missions which have helped to bring the Gospel there, and inasmuch as the ultimate responsibility for determining its faith and practice must in the end depend, under God, long after all 'foreign' missionaries have withdrawn, on the 'natives' who have learned their Christianity from various sources, it must be our supreme aim so to train the Christians of our communion that they or their descendants may be able to make a really sound contribution to the future Church of their land, when the day of reunion comes.

For himself the present writer would like to bear witness to the fact that—apart of course from public *communio in sacris*—he has met with almost unfailing kindness, sympathy, and courtesy from the Roman Catholic missionaries, French, German, and American, as well as those of the Russian Orthodox Church, by whose side he is privileged to work at the immense field which lies open before them jointly. And he would add that, while his personal relations with the far more numerous Protestant missionaries (almost exclusively American) have been almost invariably friendly, anything in the shape of common religious action appears to be made very difficult by their entirely different standpoint. For with their dislike of and disregard for Creeds, Sacraments, Liturgical Worship, and the Apostolic Ministry, and their insistence on Sabbatarianism, Teetotalism, and Bibliolatry of the Tennessee type (varied occasionally by ultra modernism), as essentials of the spiritual life, they appear to be intent (in S. Paul's words) on ' preaching another Gospel which is not another.' But he has quite sufficient faith in the Holy Spirit to believe in His power to produce even out of such disparate elements an ultimate unity and in God's good time *omnia instaurare in Christo*.

THE COUNTRY PARISH

By John Featherstonhaugh Briscoe

XII

THE COUNTRY PARISH

IT is not easy to write in general terms of
the work of a village priest because of the
great variety of country parishes,—a much
more conspicuous variety, I think, than exists
in the case of the parishes of the towns. I
have therefore ventured in this chapter to
describe chiefly such experience as I have
gained during many years in a parish of three
hundred people on the Quantock hills.

There are many reasons for which the rector
of a country parish may consider himself a very
lucky man. In the Diocese of Manchester
two years ago there were twenty-eight parishes
in charge of a single priest, of which the population was over ten thousand. A missionary
in Central Africa will tell you he has in his vast
district more than three thousand Christians
and five thousand hearers and catechumens.

The priest of a country parish is responsible
for no larger number than he can quite adequately care for. He can ' get round his job.'
He has leisure and quiet. He has the time
to read books and to say his prayers. He has
the unusual felicity of being able to spend many

hours alone. He lives amid the constant inspiration of hills and fields and flowers. He
need never be in a hurry, yet he can find plenty
of employment for every day.

The Parishioners

The village priest is very happy in his flock.
The best representatives of our race are to be
found among country people. They are un-
spoilt by the vulgar rivalries of the suburbs
and the towns. They have the beautiful
manners and the natural dignity which go with
simple hearts. There is nothing they so much
resent as empty pretention, and they are never
guilty of it themselves. They are wonderfully loyal to their home, their village, and
their priest. They are the heirs of a great
tradition. They take their part in village life
as being always conscious of independent
rights, and this is why the population of a
village is very different from just so many
servants of the squire.

The artisans and office-boys of the cities
look down on the craftsmen of the countryside ; but the fact is you need to use far more
judgement and dexterity and intelligence and
skill in work on the land and among stock
than for the mechanical routine of offices and
factories.

Our country folk are profoundly influenced
by the atmosphere of religion. They do not
argue about it, and they do not define it, but it

is taken for granted.   It is everywhere assumed that the existence and providence of God are the background of life, and that death is the prelude to judgement.   There are many survivals from the distant past.   I have heard a cottage woman say to her daughter at the death-bed of her son : ' Don't stand at the foot of the bed, Sarah Jane ; that is where the angels will come to fetch Willy away.'   The old people will tell you that they have been accustomed from childhood to end the day with the invocation of the Evangelists :

> Matthew, Mark, Luke, and John,
> Bless the bed that I lie on.

There is profound reverence for the Sacraments.   I know no more moving sight than a Baptism or Marriage or Confirmation or Easter Communion in a village church, because of the recollection and self-forgetfulness of those who take part in the rite.

The text of the Prayer Book is very familiar. Nearly always you will find a sick person ready and able to join in the prayers you say for him. The rhythm and cadence of the words are deeply loved, even if sometimes the meaning is only vaguely understood.

THE NEW RECTOR

It was noted of the saintly Bishop Challoner by one who knew him well that his behaviour

to his flock was ' not only kind but respectful.' [1]
A new rector, on arrival in a country parish,
will probably find much that is unsatisfactory
in the ecclesiastical arrangements. I do not
think any better advice can be given him than
to imitate this attitude of gentle respectfulness
in inaugurating any changes he may wish to
make. Country people inherit a tradition of
religion from the centuries of the past, which
deserves delicate and reverent consideration.
If it is desired to teach them what is new, the
new doctrine or practice must be shown to be
congruous with what they believe already. The
squire and the farmers and the peasants are
probably alike in that they are entirely without
such historical and theological knowledge or
imagination as shall enable them to appreciate
the arguments for a brand new ' Anglo-Catholic
Position.' But they will understand if they
are told that the church should be as orderly
and beautiful as the best house in the parish;
and that it is a duty to keep carefully such
Prayer Book rules as that ' the chancels shall
remain as they have done in times past,' that
the vestments shall ' be in use,' that feasts and
fasts ' are to be observed,' and that ' morning
and evening prayer are daily to be said throughout the year.'

An appeal to the Bible never fails. It will
not be disputed that the Communion Service

[1] Burton, *Life and Times of Bishop Challoner*, vol. i,
p. 120.

ought to have no less a place in the worship
of the parish than the ' breaking of the bread '
in the worship of the first days of the Church,
and the great texts from the Bible about the
Sacrament of Penance will suggest that here is
supplied a need of their own souls.

The worst way of proceeding is to empty
the church of the accustomed worshippers by
immediately making drastic and revolutionary
changes, in dependence on half a dozen im-
ported sympathizers or a batch of children.
The new rector must be quite determined to
carry with him all, or very nearly all, the
Church people of the parish ; and if he is
patient and gentle he will succeed in doing so.
Country people are very quick to respect conscience and principle and knowledge, and if
their priest can convince them that he is acting
according to his conscience, on a sound principle, and with adequate and definite knowledge, the battle will be won.

The religion of the parish, then, is to be
arranged in line with the Gospel and the
Church of England. Such customs of the
universal Church as fasting Communion and
prayer for the dead and invocation of the
Blessed Virgin and the saints may well be
commended, but the primary emphasis in the
teaching of the priest must be very plainly set
on what is central in the Christian Faith.

The church itself, dominating the parish,
preaches splendidly the majestic supremacy of

God. Jesus must be continually proclaimed
as the Son and the Word, the Interpreter and
the Messenger of the Father : the Victim
and the Saviour. The presence of the Holy
Spirit in the Church must be often explained :
the exercise of our religion is not primarily to
recall what happened in the past, but to bring
the living Christ into personal touch with every
soul, and every department of contemporary
life. The holy Church is the instrument by
which His ministries of the Gospel are to be
continued to the end of time.[1] Whether Peter
or Paul or Judas is the visible minister of the
Sacrament, writes S. Augustine, it is really
Christ Who baptizes in every case.[2] Alike at
the font and the altar and the confessional, He
whom the faithful find is Jesus Himself.

A country priest must not be content if he is
able to win from his flock no more than a dull
and patient acquiescence. He must try so to
inspire and instruct his people that among them
may be found many brave and keen apostles of
the Faith. If the parish is to be truly converted
and to exert a right influence around, it will be
due most of all to the influence of the women
and children in the homes, of one or two

[1] ' Je prends comme formule intégrale du christianisme :
" Dieu dans le Christ, et le Christ dans l'Eglise : . . . je ne
trouve la plénitude du christianisme que dans le catholicisme,
l'Eglise n'étant au fond que l'Evangile continué à travers les
siècles." '—M. Edouard le Roy, *Demain*, Oct. 26, 1906,
p. 11.

[2] S. Augustine *in Joan. Evang. Tract.* vi. 7.

farmers and labourers among the rest, of a footman or a nursery-maid in the servants' hall. The priest will work hard to form such apostles, —men, women, children, of every class—who shall be ready and able to defend religion when it is attacked, to explain it when it is misunderstood, and to proclaim, more by their lives than by their words, the power and joy and peace which the practice of a valid religion gives.

I remember how once on a journey to Plymouth a lad in the Navy told me that questions of religion were often discussed in his mess, and that he was able to silence all objectors on the strength of an accurate and exhaustive knowledge of the *Penny Catechism*.

A friend of mine was once eating his luncheon at the 'Farmer's Ordinary' on a market-day in Taunton, and was delighted to hear a young farmer make an excellent defence of the Eucharist as the right service for Sunday morning.

The Village Church

No country in the world has such delightful village churches as England, and the village priest finds the care of the fabric and furniture of his church among the most pleasant of his duties. 'The Country Parson,' wrote George Herbert, 'hath a special care of his Church, that all things there be decent, and befitting His name by which it is called.' [1]

[1] *A Priest to the Temple*, xiii.

He is fortunate if his church has escaped a drastic restoration in the Victorian age. However that may be, he will set himself now to preserve every fragment that remains of historical or artistic interest.

The three chief needs of a church are space, whitewash, and colour.

A far greater improvement is generally made by the removal of modern choir stalls blocking a small chancel, a modern brass lectern, or modern brass Communion rails, than by any addition. A mediaeval church cries out for an altar arranged in the ancient way ; a great altar, with a fine window for a reredos, and silver candlesticks, and silk hangings as bright and rich as can be got.

The next step should be the restoration of the Christ with Mary and John to the beam or screen in the chancel arch : large, solemn images, painted and gilt, wonderfully dignify and dominate a church. The organ should be in the west gallery, and this gallery can be made a beautiful feature, with a front of fretwork carved by the village boys. The font is much improved by an elaborate cover tapering upwards to a golden dove ; and the white walls of the nave make an excellent background for such pictures as are supplied by the Medici Society, whose frames are as decorative as the pictures.

The adornment of the church should be the concern of all the parishioners. In the church

I serve the riddel-posts for the altar were made by my friend at the ' Rising Sun,' the image of our Lady was given by the estate carpenter, the banner by the squire's housekeeper, the lace for the altar was sent by a Bagborough lad from ' Somewhere in France,' the great images on the rood-beam were the memorial of the parish for our five boys who were killed in the war.

The interest of the parishioners in the fabric of the church is quickened and encouraged if questions about it are discussed by the Parochial Church Council, but where matters of art and archaeology are concerned, the decision ought to be made by those who have the best knowledge about the matter.

The country priest will usually of necessity be his own sacristan. No decorations are effective unless the church is exquisitely clean and tidy. Everything about the altar must be absolutely spotless—the chalice, the linen, the candlesticks. Flowers are best kept off the altar, and arranged in groups on the floor on either side. They must be always perfectly fresh ; and the wafer-bread, the ' white ' wine, the beeswax candles and the incense should be of the best quality, and the liturgical books well printed and well bound.

The outside of most village churches is spoilt by vulgar and incongruous grave-stones. White marble never looks well, and polished granite is hardly more satisfactory. Local stone or slate should be used, and the design of the monuments should be the work of the architect who is responsible for the church. In this matter the influence and authority of the rector count for much. I have found it fairly easy to prevent the erection of unsuitable monuments in my churchyard.

THE SERVICES

The chief service of the week will be on Sunday morning at eleven. An earlier hour is impossible for people who have children, but no servants, and who live at some distance from the church. The bells are rung, and then, as Bishop Wilberforce suggested in his charge of 1866, the Litany is said, followed by the Communion Service, said and sung as it stands in the Prayer Book, with the sermon in the appointed place. After the Litany a hymn is sung, during which the priest puts on his chasuble over the alb and stole he has worn before. There is no better music for the Creed than the tune to which it was sung universally over Western Europe from the time when it began to be used in the Mass till about the Reformation. Mr. Croft has provided us with simple and religious music for the *Gloria in excelsis* ; in Advent and Lent the *Gloria* should be said, and the answers to the Commandments are always better said than sung.

It is quite necessary that the service should

be done by the time the clock is striking twelve.

The Communions of the people will be made at an earlier hour when they can come fasting: once a month and on the great feasts there should be a Mass said not later than seven. Frequent Communion has never been usual among the laity of the Church of England, and I think we must be reluctantly content if a large number of our village people are present every Sunday at the Eucharist for worship and remembrance ; and if they come ' holy and clean ' to receive Communion in fairly large numbers monthly, and in very large numbers on the great feasts of the year.

I do not consider it a disadvantage that the prayers in our rite suggest the communion of all present. Such prayers are characteristic of all the great liturgies (notably the Roman), and it is good to be reminded that the communion of those present at the Mass is the constant ideal of the Church, and was the actual practice for many centuries.

Whatever may be said about the excellence of Matins, there is no doubt that it should not take the place of Mass as the central worship of Sunday ; and also there is no doubt that it cannot be combined with Mass so as to make a liturgical service which can be done within an hour. Inevitably in a country parish the priest must be prepared usually to say Matins alone.

Evensong, as it stands in the Prayer Book, is an admirable devotion for Sunday night. The priest should take great pains to read the Lessons very well. The service may conclude with some such hymn as Bishop Woodford's translation of *Adoro te devote*,[1] sung kneeling as a salutation to our Lord in the Holy Sacrament, which should be reserved for the needs of the sick either in a swathed pyx above the angels of the altar, or in a *loculus in muro*, for which Mr. Edmund Bishop has made a learned defence.[2]

The perpetual reservation of the Sacrament in a village church is not only necessary to meet the sudden needs of the sick; it is necessary also if Communion is to be given to such people as farm-workers and footmen and kitchen-maids who cannot come at the time of service.

As soon as may be—the time depends on the circumstances of the parish—but as soon as may be, the rector decides the details of the services and the ceremonies. Everything is to be gained by inaugurating a fixed order and system. Country people keenly resent constant changes; they expect some changes with the new clergyman, and when he has made such changes as seem right and necessary, they will thank him most for keeping to what he has begun.

It is easy to make the mistake of introducing

[1] *Hymns Ancient and Modern*, 312.
[2] *Liturgica historica*, ii.

enough ceremonial to disturb the more conservative parishioners, but not enough to inspire any one with the ideal of Catholic worship. My own plan has been to make the morning service on the great feasts as magnificent as possible, with incense and cloth of gold and many lights about the altar, after the fashion of the Abbey Church of Westminster : and to use at Evensong on these few days a cope and incense for the *Magnificat*. On ordinary Sundays we use no incense, and no cope for the Litany ; and Evensong is sung as simply as in any church in England.

It is quite a mistake to suppose that ceremonial is unpopular with country people. On one occasion when I was away on a mission I had to arrange for the funeral of the little daughter of a leading farmer in the parish. I asked an elderly clergyman of the ' old school ' to officiate, knowing that he was a friend of the family. I found when I returned from the mission that the services of the elderly clergyman had been scornfully rejected ; a High Church clergyman had been found ; and the child's funeral had been done with all the honours of hymns and incense and cope and lights.

SERMONS

George Herbert was perfectly right when he spoke of preaching as one of the great opportunities of the country parson. ' The pulpit is his joy and his throne.' [1]   It is rare to find any one in a village who is much given to the reading of books, and I think it always happens that a country parson, who takes pains to preach as well as he can, is sure of an eager and attentive audience.

When he preacheth, he procures attention by all possible art : . . . by earnestness of speech ; it being natural to men to think, that where is much earnestness, there is somewhat worth hearing. . . . Sometimes he tells them stories, and sayings of others, according as his text invites him : for them men also heed, and remember better than exhortations ; which, though earnest, yet often die with the sermon, especially with country people ; which are thick, and heavy, and hard to raise to a point of zeal and fervency, and need a mountain of fire to kindle them ; but sayings and stories they will well remember. . . . By these and other means the Parson procures attention ; but the character of his sermon is HOLINESS. He is not witty, or learned, or eloquent, but HOLY : . . . and this is gained by chusing texts of devotion, not controversy ; moving and ravishing texts, whereof the Scriptures are full : and by an often urging of the presence and majesty of God.

Here is advice that cannot be bettered to-day. But when Herbert goes on to say ' the Parson exceeds not an hour in preaching,' my suggestion would rather be that he exceed not a quarter of that time on Sunday morning, and seldom attain to half of it on Sunday night.

If you glance through the book of sermon records in a village church, you will probably think that the subjects are often futile and disconnected.   It is not easy for any one to

[1] *A Priest to the Temple*, vii.

produce more than one hundred discourses every year for the same people, all of which shall be alike pious and brilliant and fresh.

A good plan is to arrange a scheme of sermons for the Sunday mornings or Sunday nights during two years, which shall cover the outline of the Christian religion. The Creed and the Commandments provide subjects for a year ; the ' Our Father ' and the Sacraments for a second year. Or you may preach for two months on the attributes of God and the Holy Trinity ; then for two months on our Lord Jesus Christ ; then for two months on the gifts and graces of the Holy Spirit. The subjects of the sermons for the following two or four months may be posted up in the church porch. In this way you secure that the regular attendants at Mass or Evensong receive some instruction on every part of the Christian religion.

No preacher should be in difficulty about a subject. Nothing is more useful than plain exposition of the Holy Scriptures ; and we have, I suppose, the best of all modern commentaries ready to our hands in English, with Loisy and Lagrange to turn to sometimes for fresh suggestions.

An anonymous journalist, in a recent book on country life, cites as a crowning example of the imbecility of a village clergyman that he preached about the importance of reunion with the Eastern Church. As often in his book, the anonymous journalist could not be more wrong. It is an excellent plan to try in your sermon to stir the villagers to think beyond the horizon of the parish, and to take such an interest in the fortunes of the Church everywhere in the world as shall be translated into prayer and work and alms.

A village congregation prefers a preacher who uses no notes. The form of his sermon may be in consequence rough and colloquial, but much is gained in simple directness.

'For myself,' said Dr. Newman, 'I think it no extravagance to say that a very inferior sermon, delivered without book, answers the purposes for which all sermons are delivered more perfectly than one of great merit, if it be written and read. . . . Eloquence, I repeat, is a gift; but most men, unless they have passed the age for learning, may with practice attain such fluency in expressing their thoughts as will enable them to convey and manifest to their audience that earnestness and devotion to their object, which is the life of preaching,—which both covers, in the preacher's own consciousness, the sense of his own deficiencies, and makes up for them over and over again in the judgement of his hearers.' [1]

The School

The village priest has probably the invaluable right of teaching religion every morning to the children in the parish school. If he misses on Monday, he will have the Scouts in the dinner hour for games and instruction. Every other morning he will use his privilege, and he will

[1] *Idea of a University*, p. 427.

spare no pains to make the lessons he gives as interesting as possible. Pictures are much help towards explaining the Bible stories. The 'Acts' become tales of thrilling adventure if the priest is familiar with Father Rackham's commentary.

There is nothing to bind him to the limits of the diocesan syllabus. The children should be taught about the ways and history of the Church, the stories of the martyrs, the work of the missionaries. They should know about the local saints, and there is much to be told in a parish like this, from which can be seen over the marshes the Tor of Glastonbury.

It is useful to set the older children once a week to write an essay on a lesson you have given them : and if the priest corrects the essay with each child alone, he helps the teachers, and widens the child's education, and wins the commendation of His Majesty's Inspector.

On the first Sunday after my arrival here I said to one small boy of the choir that he had been talking during the service. 'You be a liar' was the sulky reply. I think village boys are most successfully civilized by being made Scouts. The rector may be only an inefficient Scout-master ; but the ideals of the Scout law are excellent, and the uniform and badges link the boys of a remote village with a world-wide brotherhood beyond.

I am continually grateful to Canon Peter

U

Green for a word in one of his books which exactly defines the right attitude of a priest towards his boys. He is to behave to them ' like an Indian prince.' It could not be more happily said. You are to be kind and friendly and fatherly, but at the same time to keep a dignity and aloofness which must never be infringed. When a priest begins to pet his children, his influence with them is ruined, and the honour of his priesthood is in the dirt.

Visiting

There is no severer test of a village priest than his attitude towards visiting his flock. It is a bad sign if he finds it a labour and a bore. He ought to return from an afternoon of visits cheered and heartened and interested by all the pleasant things he has heard and seen. Each cottage home has its special character. Everywhere the rector is sure of a welcome. He is admitted to the family circle. He is spared no detail of the innermost complaints. He is told all the most intimate news. He is given to read the letter that has come from Fred in India or George in Canada.

The priest's visits should never be a nuisance to the parishioners. He will therefore avoid Mondays and Saturdays : and be very ready to say he will come another day if he finds the mother of the family more than usually busy. Each house should be visited every two months, including the servants' hall at the house of the squire.

Every visit he makes gives the priest an opportunity of influence. It is for him, as Dr. Bigg said, ' to uphold a high standard and a fine tone in everything, not only in worship and its accessories, not only in faith and morals, but in manners, in speech, in dress, in everything.' [1]

SOCIAL CONDITIONS

The social conditions of most village parishes have enormously improved during the last twenty years. When I came first to Bagborough, it was quite common to find children in October whose underclothes were ' sewn on for the winter.' Now there is scarcely a child who is not warmly clad and perfectly clean. One great gain of the war was that it introduced the young men of the countryside to the joys of a bath.

Twenty years ago in this parish there were no amusements except a club-day once a year, which began with a service and procession, and ended in what was called a dance, but was more like a drunken brawl, in a dimly lighted ' barton.' One of the first things I did was to teach the lads how to waltz and to find some one to teach the girls. Now we have an excellent parish hall, with frequent dances and whist-drives of the utmost elegance and pro-

[1] *The Spirit of Christ in Common Life*, p. 92.

priety. The parish hall is the property of the rector and the churchwardens, but it is managed entirely by a committee elected at an annual meeting open to all parishioners.

I do not think it is good for the village priest to be in conspicuous alliance with any political party. His characteristic work is to draw together the various classes of the community. It is excellent for all to meet in their best clothes at parish parties ; and when the squire and the farmers and the labourers are accustomed to kneel side by side in their common home, they learn to see in each other fellow members of the one body of Christ, and so conscience is quickened about wages and housing and work.

The priest should try to be the friend of all alike. If he lives alone in a very simple way, he will be accessible to everybody ; and it will be easy for any one, however shy, to come to see him. All will be sure of a welcome, whether he is a young labourer going to get married, or off to Canada, or whether he is the squire's son, home from Eton or Sandhurst.

CONFESSION

A letter of John Keble, written between the years 1840 and 1850, bitterly deplores the evils resulting from the disuse of Confession in a country parish :

' It is sad to think,' he writes, ' how very little one knows of one's people. We go on working in the dark, and in the dark it will be, until the rule of systematic Confession is revived in our Church. This is one of the things which make persons like Mr. Gladstone, however competent in most respects, yet on the whole incompetent judges of the real working of our English system. They do not, they cannot, unless they were tried as we are, form an adequate notion, how absolutely we are in our parishes like people whose lantern has blown out, and who are feeling their way, and continually stepping into puddles and splotches of mud, which they think are dry stones. Then the tradition which goes by the name of Justification by Faith, and which in reality means that one who has sinned and is sorry for it, is as if he had not sinned, blights and benumbs one in every limb, in trying to make people aware of their real state. These are the sort of things, and not the want of handsome Churches, and respect for Church Authority, and such like comparatively external points, which make me at times feel so disheartened about our system altogether, and cause a suspicion, against one's will, that the life is gone or going out of it. And this is why I so deprecate the word and the idea of Protestantism, because it seems inseparable to me from " Every man his own absolver " ; that is, in other words, the same as " Peace where there is no peace," and mere shadows of Repentance.' [1]

The Sacrament of Penance is a very important part of the spiritual apparatus of every Catholic parish. One of the best tests of the vitality of a priest's work is whether after some years he is still hearing first confessions from his parishioners. There are some in every place who are unhappy because of an old sin—often sin before marriage—and they will be very glad to come to Confession to get rid of that special burden, even if they do not form the

Letters of Spiritual Counsel, xix.

habit of making their confessions at regular intervals afterwards.

Many young men and women were guilty of grave sins during the feverish excitement of the years of war and the months that followed ; they greatly need the opportunity of Confession so that they may start their religious life afresh with a clean sheet.

A bad fault of Victorian times (is it an extinct fault to-day ?) was carelessness about approach to Communion. It was not unusual to arrive at church for Morning Prayer and ' stay behind for the second service ' with no previous preparation whatever. The exhortations in the Communion Service contain excellent teaching about the reverence due to the Holy Sacrament: the communicant is to come ' holy and clean ' to the ' heavenly feast, in the marriage garment required by God in holy Scripture.' There are many in every parish who will be glad to make their confession before the great feasts that they may be sure their souls are ' holy and clean,' ready to receive our Lord.

The village priest must be prepared to find that not seldom he will be told by his penitent ' I have not done anything particularly wrong, but I want to make sure I am going to Communion all right.' It is exactly the case carefully provided for by S. Thomas Aquinas : ' *ille, qui non habet mortalia, non tenetur ad confessionem venialium, sed sufficit ad praeceptum ecclesiae implendum ut se sacerdoti repraesentet, et se osten-*

*dat absque conscientia mortalis esse ; et hoc ei
pro confessione reputatur.'* [1]

Country people are delightfully simple and
natural about their confessions. On a wintry
evening soon after I had come here three
farm boys arrived at my cottage saying that
they wanted me to forgive them their sins,
but might they please come altogether. So I
listened to the story of their sins as they knelt
side by side by the fire in my study.

There was an old policeman in the parish
who could not make up his mind to come to
the Sacraments. However, one Christmas-
time he came to Confession and Communion,
and on his return home he said to his daughter,
' I do feel so good : I should like to die.' They
found him in his chair a few days after, dead in
his sleep.

I had a great friend in the village blacksmith :
a charming young man, and our champion
boxer. He used to come to Mass and Communion, but did not make his confession until
a few days before his death. I was told afterwards that when I had left him, he announced
to his astonished family that now he was perfectly happy, because he was sure that all his
sins were forgiven.

Sometimes a labourer will stop me in the
road—' I want to come and talk to you about
my sins.' And once I was walking in my
garden when a strange old peasant appeared,

[1] *Summa Theologica*, III, *supplem. quaest.* vi, *art.* 3.

who said he had come from a village on the other side of the Quantocks, and could I tell him how he might have his sins forgiven ?

It is a wise plan to wait in church in the place where confessions are heard for at least an hour on two evenings every week, and much more often before the great feasts. Again and again it will happen that the person in the parish you least expect to see, is there kneeling by your side.

There must be no mystery about Confession. It should be as entirely normal and familiar in the religious system of the parish as Baptism or Communion. While it is the best plan to hear all confessions in church, it may easily happen that some men and lads prefer to come to the priest's house for their confessions late in the evening. For these occasions it is convenient if the priest's study has a door opening into his garden, so that those who come to see him may escape the scrutiny of his house-keeper.

The Priest Himself

The leisure, which is the happy opportunity of the village priest, should ensure first of all that he is diligent about his prayers. Early every morning he will be at the altar to offer the Holy Sacrifice, with the thought in his mind that he does not do so only for himself : ' *sacerdos in persona omnium offert et sumit.*' [1] He is the representative of all in the parish to-day ; and

---

[1] S. Thomas, *Summa Theologica*, III, *quaest.* lxxx, *art.* 12.

he bears in his heart all the needs of all the world as he stands before the Throne.

It is convenient for him to combine his meditation with his Mass before breakfast, when he can count on being undisturbed. An hour then, and another hour round about Evensong, will give him time for his prayers ; and the people in the parish will soon understand when they may be sure to find him in church. If Matins of the following day is said overnight in accordance with the usual Latin custom, the priest will escape the danger of being hurried in his devotions, which should be finished before he has his breakfast, and goes to his school at nine.

An annual retreat of not less than three clear days is all but a necessity for a village priest who desires to persevere in the spirit of his vocation. The fact that he lives so much alone, with so little from outside to stimulate and help him, and the fact that the whole religious atmosphere of the parish depends in so large a measure on himself, makes his need of a good retreat quite imperative.

The country priest may sometimes be tempted to think of his work as being very futile and insignificant. M. Yves le Querdec [1] has perhaps best described how such ministry among simple peasants may be enterprised and carried through in a spirit of high religious consecration. For myself, there are no words

[1] *Lettres d'un Curé de Campagne.*

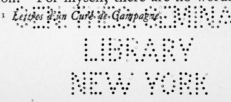

I remember more happily than those with which Lord Alwyne Compton, gentlest and humblest of bishops, sent me to my parish : 'It may be said,' he wrote, 'there is not enough for you to do. I never admit that view—if you can bring a hundred souls to glory it is a good work.'

Printed by A. R. Mowbray & Co. Ltd.
London and Oxford

1921